The
SECRET OF HAPPY CHILDREN

The
SECRET *of*
~: HAPPY ~
CHILDREN

WHY CHILDREN BEHAVE THE WAY THEY DO—
AND WHAT YOU CAN DO TO HELP THEM TO BE
OPTIMISTIC, LOVING, CAPABLE AND HAPPY

STEVE BIDDULPH

ILLUSTRATIONS BY ALLAN STOMANN

✦

MARLOWE & COMPANY
NEW YORK

Thanks to all in the Transactional Analysis community from the early seventies onward, especially Colin McKenzie, Pat McKenzie, the Maslens, the Mellors, and Jean Grigor. These people saved my life and started me traveling down this wonderful road. To my wise and straight-talking partner Shaaron Biddulph. To Wanda Whitely and Rex Finch, long-term editors and friends. And to all parents everywhere, for their courage and for still remembering how to laugh.

Contents

✦

Contents

The Story Behind This Book

✦

When I FIRST wrote *The Secret of Happy Children*, I never dreamed that it would take off in quite the way it has. Fourteen years after first firing up the typewriter, it has been read by over a million people, in seventeen languages.

Back then I was just a beginning family therapist, with a heartfelt wish to make it easier for fathers and mothers to get along well with their kids, and for kids to live without the put-downs and fears that our generation often felt.

The first edition announced on the opening page that I had no children, only wombats (and that these were quite badly behaved!). I mentioned this because it was true, and because I wanted my readers to take everything I said with a grain of salt—to trust their own judgment. I still believe this—experts are a hazard to your family! If you listen to your own heart it will always tell you what the best way is to raise your children. Books, experts, and friends help you only if they take you closer to your own good sense.

I do have kids of my own now, almost raised in fact, and the wombats have long grown up! But my feelings haven't changed. I still get a melting feeling in my chest when I see a young mother with a new baby, or a young father playing with his kids.

I'm more impressed by young parents and their efforts than by any sports hero, rock star, or business tycoon!

Anyhow, I'm proud to be launching this U.S edition. Many hundreds of parents have told me that they found the ideas in this book powerful and helpful. It's grown and improved with their feedback over the years.

I hope you like it too.

Foreword

✦

Why ARE SO many adults unhappy? Think of all the people you know who have problems—who lack confidence, cannot make a decision, can't relax, or can't make friends with other people. Think of those who are aggressive, putting people down and ignoring the needs of those around them. Add to the above all those just holding on until the next drink or the next tranquilizer.

In one of the richest countries in the world, unhappiness is epidemic. One adult in every five will at some time need psychiatric care, one marriage in two ends in divorce, one adult in four needs medication to relax. It's a great life!

Unemployment and difficult economic times don't help, but unhappiness is present in all income groups—rich, poor, and in between. It's a problem, in fact, that no amount of money seems to solve.

On the plus side, we are often struck by some people's constant cheerfulness and optimism. Why is it that, in some individuals, the human spirit blossoms in spite of apparent hardship?

The simple fact is many people have unhappiness programmed into them. They have been unwittingly taught as children to be unhappy, and are now living out the script. Through reading this book you may discover that, by accident, you are hypnotizing your children into disliking themselves, and causing them to have problems that may last a lifetime.

But this need not be so. You can program your children to be optimistic, loving, capable, and happy. To have a good chance of a long, successful life. So let's begin . . .

The
SECRET OF HAPPY CHILDREN

·∵ **one** ·~

Seeds in the Mind

YOU HYPNOTIZE YOUR CHILDREN EVERY SINGLE DAY.
YOU MAY AS WELL DO IT PROPERLY!

◆

It's NINE O'CLOCK at night and I'm sitting in my office with a tearful fifteen-year-old girl. She is wearing makeup and is dressed in fashionable, older-than-her-years clothes, but the effect is only to make her look more helpless and childlike. She and I are talking about the fact that she is pregnant and what can be done about it.

This is familiar ground for me, and for anyone who works with teenagers. It doesn't mean, though, that it can be hurried. What matters is that, for the young woman sitting in front of me, this is the worst day of her life and she needs all the support, time, and clarity that I can muster. Above all she must make her own right decision.

I ask about her parents' likely reaction—when they find out. She almost spits out the answer.

"Oh, they'll say they told me so. They always said I'd never amount to nuthin'!"

3

Later, as I drive home, that one sentence stays in my mind. "They always said I'd never amount to nothing." I've often heard parents talk to kids like that.

"You're hopeless."
"God, you're a nuisance."
"You'll be sorry, just you see."
"You're as bad as your uncle Merv" (who's in jail).
"You're just like your auntie Eve" (who's fond of a drink).
"You're crazy, do you hear?"

This is the kind of programming that many youngsters grow up with; it is passed on unthinkingly by stressed-out parents and continues as a kind of family curse down the generations. It's called a *self-fulfilling prophecy* because saying it often enough makes it come true. Children, with their brilliant, perceptive ways, will usually live up to our expectations!

These are extreme examples, which we'd all recognize immediately as destructive. Most negative programming, however, is much more subtle. Observe children playing in a vacant lot, climbing trees. "You'll fall! Watch out! You'll slip!" cries the voice of their anxious mother from over the fence.

The half-drunk father ends a halfhearted argument with his wife, who goes off in a "huff" to buy some cigarettes. "There y'are son, never trust a woman. They'll just use y'up." The seven-year-old looks up solemnly and nods. Yes, Dad.

And, in a million living rooms and kitchens:

"God, you're lazy."
"You're so selfish."
"You silly idiot, stop that."
"Dumb."

"Give it to me, stupid."
"Don't be such a pest."

This kind of talk doesn't just make a child feel bad momentarily. Put-downs also have a hypnotic effect and act unconsciously, like seeds in the mind, seeds that will grow and shape the child's self-image, eventually becoming part of his personality.

How Do We Hypnotize Our Children?

HYPNOSIS AND SUGGESTION have long been a source of fascination to people. They seem slightly mystical and unreal and yet are well accepted scientifically. Most people have witnessed them, perhaps as part of a stage show, or in getting help to stop smoking, or on a relaxation tape.

We are familiar with the key elements of hypnosis: the use of some device to distract the mind ("Vatch ze vatch"), the commanding tone ("You are feeling sleepy!"), and the rhythmic, repetitious tone of the hypnotist's speech ("Hey! Wake up!"). We also know about post-hypnotic suggestion, the ability to implant a command that the unsuspecting person later carries out, often to his or her dismay, at a given signal. It all makes for good theater, but also for excellent therapy in the hands of a qualified practitioner.

What most people don't realize, though, is that *hypnosis is an everyday event.* Whenever we use certain patterns of speech, we reach into the unconscious minds of our children and program them, even though we have no such intention.

The old concept—that hypnosis requires an altered state of mind, or trance, has been abandoned. This is only one form of unconscious learning. The rather frightening truth is that the human mind can be programmed in normal waking life beneath the awareness of the person involved. Already in the United States, many sales and advertising people as well as lawyers are being trained in the use of hypnotic methods embedded in normal business conversation—a scary concept. Fortunately hypnosis can be countered if the subject becomes aware of the process. Accidental hypnosis, though, is part of everyday life. Parents, without realizing it, implant messages in their child's mind, and these messages, unless strongly contradicted, will echo on for a lifetime.

Hypnotized Without Knowing It

*T*HE LATE Dr. Milton Erikson was recognized as the world's foremost hypnotist. He was once called upon to treat a man who suffered extreme pain from cancer, was refusing to have hypnosis, and was not being helped by painkillers. Erikson simply stopped by the man's room and started talking about the man's hobby of growing tomatoes.

A careful listener could have detected the unusual rhythm in Erikson's speech and, the stressing of odd phrases, like "deep down" (in the soil), growing "good and strong," "easy" (to pick), "warm and loose" (in the greenhouse). Also, the observer could have noted that Erikson's face and posture changed very slightly as he spoke those key phrases. The man in question simply thought that it was a pleasant exchange. Until he died, however, five days later, as doctors knew he must, the man felt no further pain.

✦

"YOU" MESSAGES

A CHILD'S MIND is full of questions. Perhaps the greatest of these are the questions "Who am I?," "What kind of person am I?," and "Where do I fit in?" These are the questions of self-definition, or identity, upon which we base our lives as adults, and from which we make all our key decisions. A child's mind is remarkably affected by statements that begin with the words "You are . . ."

Whether the message is "You are so lazy" or "You're a great kid," these statements from the important "big" people will go deeply and firmly into the child's unconscious. I have heard so many adults, overcome by a life crisis, recalling what they were told as a child: "I'm so useless. I know I am."

Imagine how differently your child's life will turn out if he has the following beliefs about himself:

- ✦ *I am a good person.*
- ✦ *I can get along well with most people.*
- ✦ *I can usually figure things out.*
- ✦ *I have a good brain.*
- ✦ *I'm really creative.*
- ✦ *My body is healthy and strong.*
- ✦ *I like the way I look.*

. . . and so on!

Psychologists (who love to complicate things) call these statements "attributions." These attributions crop up again and again in adult life.

"Why don't you apply for that promotion?"
"No, I'm not good enough."
"But he's just like your last husband. Why did you marry him?"
"I'm just stupid, I guess."
"Why do you let them push you around like that?"
"That's the story of my life."

These words—"not good enough," "just stupid"—did not come out of the blue. They are recorded in people's brains because they were said to them at an age when they were unable to question their truthfulness. "But surely," I can hear you saying, "children must disagree with the 'you' messages they are given?"

Certainly children think about the things that are said to them, checking for accuracy. But they may have no comparisons. At times we are all lazy, selfish, untidy, stupid, forgetful, mischievous, and so on. The fire-and-brimstone preacher in the old-time church was on to a sure thing when he thundered out, "You have sinned!"—Everyone had!

"Adults know everything; they can even read your mind." Such are the thoughts of a child. So when a child is told "You're clumsy," he or she becomes nervous, and thus clumsy. The child told "You're a pest" feels the rejection, becomes desperate for reassurance, and so pesters even more. The child told "You're an idiot" may violently disagree on the outside, but inside can only sadly agree. You're the adult, so you must be right.

"You" messages work at *both* the conscious and unconscious levels. In my clinical work I've often asked children to describe themselves, and they will say things like "I'm a bad kid," or "I'm a nuisance."

Others, though, will show evidence of confusion: "Mom and Dad say they love me, but I don't think they do." Consciously they hear the words, but unconsciously they hear/see/sense a different feeling behind the words.

It's all in the way we say it. We can choose to say to children, "I'm angry with you and I want you to clean up your toys NOW!" and have no fears about lasting effects. If we say, "You lazy little brat, why don't you ever do what you're told?" and repeat this kind of message whenever conflict occurs, then the result will come as no surprise.

A special note here—sometimes parents who have read too many books on self-esteem think they have to be bright and positive all the time. This leads to falsity that a child can sense and can be just as much of a problem as being too negative. So don't pretend to be happy or loving when you aren't feeling that way—it's confusing and can make children become evasive and in time quite disturbed. We can be honest about our feelings, without putting children down. They can handle "I'm really tired today," or "Right now I'm too angry" . . . especially if this matches what their senses are telling them. It helps them realize that you are human too, which has got to be a good thing.

Being Told You Are Bad

At a large parents' meeting I once spoke to, I asked if people would call out the "you" messages they remembered hearing as children. I wrote them on a whiteboard and this is what we came up with:

You're lazy clumsy stupid
a nuisance just a girl
too young to understand
selfish dumb
a pest dirty
thoughtless inconsiderate
always late greedy
bad-tempered brainless noisy
gutless a worry crazy
mental making your mother sick
ugly plain immature
just like your father
...and on it went.

The examples came in little rushes at first, as people's memories were triggered, but by the end the whiteboard was covered and the room was almost in a state of riot. The sense of relief and release was very evident in the large hall as people spoke aloud the words that had hurt them so long ago.

Very few people felt their parents had been deliberately destructive or malicious—it was simply that this was the way children were corrected. "Tell them they're bad and that makes them good!" Those were the Dark Ages of child-rearing: we're just beginning to escape.

Your Mind Remembers Everything That Ever Happened to You

*I*n the 1950s people with epilepsy had a tough time because the medications we now use had not been developed. A scientist called Penfield found that an operation could be used to help in very severe cases. By making small cuts on the surface of a person's brain, he could sometimes reduce or even halt the "electrical storms" that caused epileptic seizures.

The interesting part—I hope you're sitting down as you read this—is that patients were required, for safety reasons, to be conscious, and the operation was done under only a local anesthetic. The surgeon removed a small piece of skull, made the incisions and then put back the piece of bone and sewed up the skin. It makes me shudder, too, but it was better than having the disease!

During the operation, the patients experienced something very surprising. As the doctor, using a fine probe, delicately touched the surface of the brain, the patient would suddenly have vivid recollections—watching *Gone with the Wind* years earlier, complete with the smell of cheap perfume in the cinema and the beehive hairstyle of the person in front! When the doctor moved the probe to another spot, the person would see before him his fourth birthday, even though he was wide awake and sitting in the operating chair. It was the same with every patient, though of course the memories were different.

Subsequent research backed up this remarkable discovery: that everything—every sight, sound, smell and spoken word—is stored forever in our brain, along with the emotions we felt at the time. It is often difficult to remember but nonetheless it is there, having its effect. On the wrinkled surface of our brain our life is recorded in its entirety!

✦

Unconscious hearing is another phenomenon that you've almost certainly experienced. You've been at a party or a meeting, listening to someone near you. The room is buzzing with people talking and perhaps music, too. Suddenly, from a conversation clear across the room, you hear someone say your name, or the name of a friend, or something that concerns you. *Aaargh!* you think, *What are they saying about me?*

How does this happen? We have discovered from research that there are two parts to your hearing: firstly, what your ears actually pick up; and secondly, what you pay conscious attention to.

Although you are unaware of it, your brilliant hearing system is filtering every conversation within range in the room and, if a key word or phrase occurs, the switchboard department in your brain "puts it through" to conscious attention. You certainly couldn't listen to all that was being said at one time but, nonetheless, a primitive filter is scanning it for important messages. We know this from many experiments and also from the fact that under hypnosis people can recall things that they *didn't consciously notice at the time!*

The following situation has been reported in many parts of the world:

> *Late one night a large truck runs out of control, careers downhill, and smashes through the front wall of a house. When rescuers enter the house they are amazed to find a young mother sleeping heavily, undisturbed by the crash. As they stand there, not knowing what to do, a baby begins to cry in the back room. The mother instantly awakes. "Wha . . . what's going on?"*
>
> *The filter in her hearing system works on as she sleeps but is checking for only one thing—the baby—and only this sound is "put through" to her awareness.*

How does all of the above relate to children? Think of all the things that are said about children when they are supposedly not listening. Then remember their acute listening powers (a lollipop wrapper at fifty yards!). We may well include the time when they are asleep, for there is clear evidence that sounds and speech are taken in even as a person dreams and sleeps.

> *Our oldest child was so active during his toddler years that there was seldom a quiet moment with him. Shaaron would sometimes wait until he lay peacefully asleep, and then sit at his bedside, stroke him, and tell him how beautiful and loved he was. It was the only time he stayed still enough to do it!*

Also, there is that obvious time when a toddler has not yet started to say many words, but understands an enormous amount of what is being said. Watch out for this—they are listening big time!

I am often amazed by parents who have been fighting bitterly for years, or are desperately unhappy, for some reason telling me, "Of course, the kids know nothing about it." Children, in fact, know almost everything about everything. They may oblige you by keeping it to themselves or only show it indirectly by bed-wetting or trying to murder their siblings, but they know. So, if you talk about your children, be sure you are saying what you really want to say. This, too, is a direct channel to their minds.

And why not start to use this channel to boost them by saying what you genuinely like and appreciate to others while they're in earshot? This is especially useful at ages/stages when direct praise is embarrassing to them.

Hearing and Healing

*T*HIS STORY is told by one of my teachers, Dr. Virginia Satir.

A child had just been operated on for tonsil removal and, back in the ward, was failing to stop bleeding. Dr. Satir joined the concerned staff in discussing what they sould do.

On an impulse, she asked what was happening in the theater at the time of the operation.

"Oh, we'd just finished a throat cancer operation on an old lady."

"What were you talking about?"

"Oh, that last operation, and how she didn't have much of a chance of living—there was too much damage."

Dr. Satir's mind worked fast. She saw the child undergoing the simple and routine procedure, under general anesthetic, while the staff talked about the previous patient: "not much chance of living," "pretty bad shape."

Quickly, she asked that the child be taken back to the theater. She instructed the staff as to what to say:

"Gee, this kid looks good and healthy, not like the old lady we operated on before."

"This kid has a nice healthy throat."

"She'll be healed in a jiffy and back playing with her friends!"

The bleeding stopped and the child went home the next day.

✦

ADDING POWER TO OUR MESSAGE

SCIENTISTS HAVE ALSO found that a message is about five times stronger if it is accompanied by nonverbal signals that reinforce it such as touch, eye contact, or strength and tone of voice.

This is really quite simple.

If a person says to you, "You're a pest!" you will probably feel somewhat insulted. If he says it with a frown and a loud voice, this will be worse.

If he says it very loudly, moves toward you while making menacing gestures and appears somewhat out of control, then you have a problem.

If he happens to be three times larger than you and is one of your family—on whom your well-being depends—you will probably remember the incident for the rest of your life.

Modern-day men and women (especially those of Anglo-Saxon descent) tend to be constrained in our emotional expression. We do not act or speak with very much passion or force. We tend to keep our good and bad feelings to ourselves and, when things go badly, we try to carry the burden without giving any outward signs.

Because of this, our children may live in a situation where day-to-day messages are fairly vague and indirect: "Now don't do that, darling, it's time to go," "That's a good boy." Both positive and negative messages are casual and not great in their impact.

Then, one day, when life has really overloaded Mom or Dad, there comes a powerful outburst—"You little brat, I wish you'd shut up!"—accompanied by wild eyes, sudden, close proximity, ear-splitting volume, and a sense of quivering lack of control that is unforgettable. The message is inescapable, although untrue: "This is what Mom or Dad *really* thinks of me!"

The words that overwrought parents choose at these times can be remarkably strong:

> *"I wish you'd never been born."*
> *"You're a stupid, stupid child."*
> *"You're killing me, do you hear?"*
> *"I'd like to throttle you!"*

It's not bad to get angry at or around children. On the contrary, children need to learn that people can be angry and discharge tension and be heard, all in complete safety. Elizabeth Kubler Ross taught that real anger lasts twenty seconds and is mostly noise. The problem comes when the positive messages ("You are great," "We love you," "We'll look after you") are not equally strong or frequent. Often, although we feel many positive things about our children, we do not communicate them.

Almost every child is dearly loved, but many children do not know this; many adults will go to their graves still believing that they were a nuisance and a disappointment to their parents. It is one of the most moving moments in family therapy to be able to clear away this misunderstanding between parent and child.

At the times when a child's life goes wobbly—when a new baby is brought home, if a marriage breaks up, if they fail a test at school, or there is no work for a hopeful teenager—it is important to give positive messages, anchored with a hand on a shoulder and a clear look in the eye: whatever happens, you are special and important to us. We know you're great.

WHAT *NOT* TO DO

So far we've talked about the unconscious programming of children to be unhappy adults. There are lots of direct ways that this happens, too! Here's how to avoid these.

When disciplining, don't use put-downs when a simple demand would do.

Don't even use put-downs in a friendly way, say, as a nickname.

Hey, elephants ears! Dinner's ready

Don't compare!

You're as bad as your father

Why can't you be sweet and good like your baby brother?

Set an example!

Will you relax!

You hit him again and I'll KILL you

Never talk to other people about your children's faults within their earshot.

Don't take pride in patterns that are bound to cause trouble later.

Don't use guilt to control children.

These sorts of statements can be left out of your parenting repertoire for good. You and your children will feel better for it.

The Way You Say It—
Positive Wording Makes
Competent Kids

*A*S ADULTS, we guide our own behavior and feelings by "self-talk," the chatter that goes on inside our heads. ("Better not forget to get gas," "Oh hell, I forgot my purse, I must be getting senile," etc.) Self-talk is learned directly from parents and teachers. With your own kids, self talk offers a great chance to share all sorts of useful data that they can internalize – and use all their lives.

For example, we can say to a child, "Don't you dare get into any fights at school today!" or we can say "I want you to have a good time at school today and only play with the kids you like."

Why should such a small thing make a difference? It's all in the way the human mind works. If someone offered you a million dollars not to think of a blue monkey for two minutes, you wouldn't be able to do it! (Try it now if you don't believe us!) If a child is told "Don't fall out of the tree," then he has to think two things: "Don't" and "fall out of the tree." When we think of an action, we automatically rehearse the action with our mental imagery, and even with small movements of our muscles. (Imagine biting hard into a lemon, and notice how you react to just the fantasy!) A child who is vividly imagining falling out of a tree probably will. Far better to use positive wording: "Look for a strong branch to put your foot."

There are dozens of chances each day to get this right. Rather than say "Don't run out into the traffic," it's easier and better to say "Stay on the sidewalk close to me," or "Hang on to my hand," so that the child imagines what TO do, and not what NOT to do.

Give kids clear instructions as to the right way to do things. Kids don't always know how to be safe, so make your commands specific: "Tracey, hold on to the side of the boat with both your hands" is much more useful than "Don't you dare fall out" or, worse still, "How do you think I'll feel if you drown?" The changes are small but the difference is enormous.

Positive wording helps your kids to think and act positively, and to feel capable in a wide range of situations. They will imagine success and talk themselves through to good outcomes. Our encouraging words will stay with them for life.

I'll Give You Crazy!

*H*AVE YOU ever listened to yourself talking to your kids, and just moaned? A lot of the things we say to kids are, well, crazy.

Scottish comedian Billy Connolly bemoaned some of these in a recent concert we heard . . . (you'll have to imagine the accent).

"Mom, can I go to the pictures?" "Pictures! I'll give you pictures!"

"Can I have some bread then?" "Bread! I'll bread you, my boy!"

Most of us can remember being told things as a child that simply made no sense at all, phrases such as: Pull your socks up, young man . . . If you don't come to your senses soon . . . You'll smile on the other side of your face! . . . I'll teach you to make a fool of me! . . . and so on. It's no wonder some people grow up to be a little confused.

I was visiting an elementary school recently where some parents had brought their toddlers to join in a new play group. While we were waiting to start, a lively and curious little boy started to pull some math equipment off a shelf. His harassed-looking mom told him "If you touch that the teacher will cut your fingers off!" Now any of us can understand the motivation to say this kind of thing—when nothing else works, try terror! But with this kind of message coming at him, what can a child conclude about life? It can only go two ways: either the world is a crazy and dangerous place, or else, it's no good listening to Mom, she talks a load of garbage. Now there's the start of a well-adjusted life!

One day (true confession) I told my two-year-old son that the police might be cross with him if he didn't wear his seatbelt. I was hot and tired, and I hate squirming my six-foot-four frame around inside cars to fasten seatbelt buckles on protesting kids. It was a cheap stunt, and I paid the price. As soon as the words came out of my mouth I regretted it. For days after I had questions by the dozens. "Do the policeman have guns?" "Are there any policeman down this road?" It was a major job of rehabilitation to get him back to feeling calm and comfortable around the men and women in blue.

We don't always have to explain everything to our kids, or endlessly reason with them till we are blue in the face. "Because I say so" is a good enough reason some of the time. But there is nothing ever to be gained by needlessly scaring them. "When your father gets home . . ." "You'll make me so sick I'll have to go away . . ." "We'll put you into a home . . ." are the kind of messages that harm and haunt even tough children. We are their main source of information early on, and later our credibility is put to the test (since they have or will have other sources to compare us with). Our job is to give them a realistic, even slightly rosy picture of the world—which they can build on as they go, and so become hardy and secure on the inside. When they encounter trickiness or dishonesty later in life, they will at least know that this isn't completely the way of the world, that some people are trustworthy, and safe to be around—Mom and Dad included.

✦

WHY DO PARENTS PUT CHILDREN DOWN?

AT THIS POINT in the book, you could be feeling guilty about the way that you speak to your own children. Please don't—it isn't too late to change. There is plenty you can do to overcome old programming whether your children are still little or even if they are now adults.

The first step is to begin understanding yourself, to know why put-downs became part of your parenting in the first place. Almost every parent uses unnecessary put-downs from time to time. There are three main reasons for this.

1. *You repeat what was said to you!*

    You weren't taught about parenting in school. But you did have one clear example to work from—your own parents.

    I'm sure you've found yourself in a heated moment yelling at your kids and then thinking, "Good grief, that's what my parents used to say to me and I hated it!" Those old tape recordings are your "automatic pilot," however, and it takes presence of mind to stop yourself and say something else.

    Some parents, of course, go to the other extreme. With painful memories of the way in which they were raised, they swear never to scold, hit, or deprive their own children. The danger here is that they may overdo it, and their children suffer from a lack of control. It isn't easy, is it?

2. *You just thought it was the right thing to do!*

    It was once thought that kids were basically bad, and that the thing to do was to tell them how bad they were. This would shame them into being better.

    Perhaps you were brought up in this way. As a parent, you simply hadn't thought about self-esteem or the need to help children gain confidence. If so, I hope that what you are reading has changed your mind. Now that you realize how put-downs damage children, I'm sure you'll be keen to stop using them.

3. *You are "stressed out."*

When money is short, or you are overworked, lonely, or bored, then you are much more likely to be destructive in what you say to kids.

The reasons for this are clear. When we are pressured in any way, we build up a body tension that needs discharging. It actually does in the moment feel good to lash out at someone, in words or actions.

Our children often get the brunt of it because they are easier to get angry with than our spouse, boss, landlord, or whomever. It's important to think it through: I feel so tense! Who am I *really* angry with?

The relief of lashing out is short-lived, since the child is likely to behave even more badly as a result, and of course we feel awful and then get even more stressed.

If this happens, it is vitally important that you find a safe way to let off steam.

Tension can be released in two ways:

1. By vigorous action, such as hitting a mattress, doing some physical work, going for a brisk walk. This is no small matter—many a child's life has been saved by being shut in the bedroom while a distraught parent walks around the yard outside as a means of calming down.
2. By dissolving the stress through talking with a friend, finding affection from a partner (if you're fortunate enough to have one), or through some sport or activity, such as yoga, or

massage that releases the stress and allows your body to relax deeply.

Eventually as a mom or dad, you must learn to care for yourself as well as caring for your children. You actually do more for your kids by spending some time each day on your own health and relaxation than by being totally devoted to serving them every second of the day. (More about this in Chapter 8.)

So, that's the end of the bad news. The rest of this book is about how to communicate the easier way! It is possible to change, and many parents have told me that just hearing about these ideas has helped them immediately.

Already, while you've been reading, your ideas have been changing. You'll find that, without even trying, your interactions with your children will start to be easier and more positive. I promise!

~ two ~

What Children Really Want

IT'S CHEAPER THAN VIDEO GAMES,
AND HEALTHIER THAN ICE CREAM!

◆

The QUESTION THAT is uppermost in the minds of millions of parents every day can be summed up in one word . . .

Why do kids act up? Why do they always explore where they shouldn't? Why do they do things that they are not supposed to—fight, tease, disobey, provoke, argue, make a mess, and generally seem to want to persecute Mom and Dad?

Why do some kids actually seem to *enjoy* getting into trouble?

This chapter tells you what is going on inside "naughty" children, and how "bad" behavior is actually the result of good (healthy) forces going astray.

After reading this chapter, you'll be able to make more sense of children's misbehavior and you'll also know how to prevent and divert it to happier alternatives.

You don't believe me? Read on!

Children act up for one reason only: they have *unmet needs*. "But what needs," you are thinking, "do my children have that are unmet? I feed them, clothe them, buy them toys, keep them warm and clean . . ."

Well, there are some extra needs (luckily very cheap to provide) that go beyond the "basics" mentioned. These mysterious needs are essential, not only to make happy children but to maintain life itself. Perhaps I can explain it best by telling a story.

*I*N 1945, World War II ended and Europe lay in ruins. Among the many human problems to be tackled was that of caring for the thousands of orphans whose parents had been killed or permanently separated from them by the war.

The Swiss, who had managed to stay out of the war itself, sent their health workers out to begin tackling some of these problems; one man, a doctor, was given the job of researching how to best care for the orphan babies.

He traveled about Europe and visited many kinds of orphan-care situations, to see what the most successful type of care was. He saw many extremes. In some places,

American field hospitals had been set up and the babies were snug in stainless steel cots, in hygienic wards, getting their four-hourly feeds of special milk formula from crisply uniformed nurses.

At the other end of the scale, in remote mountain villages, a truck had simply pulled up, the driver had asked, "Can you look after these babies?" and left half a dozen crying infants in the care of the villagers. Here, surrounded by kids, dogs, goats, in the arms of the village women, the babies took their chances on goats' milk and the communal stewpot.

The Swiss doctor had a simple way of comparing the different forms of care. No need even to weigh the babies, let alone measure coordination or look for smiling and eye contact. In those days of influenza and dysentery he used the simplest of all statistics—the death rate.

And what he discovered was rather a surprise . . . As epidemics raged through Europe and many people were dying, the children in the rough villages were thriving better than their scientifically cared-for counterparts in the hospitals!

✦

The doctor had discovered something that old wives had known for a long time. He had discovered that babies need *love* to live.

The infants in the field hospital had everything but affection and stimulation. The babies in the villages had more hugs, bounces, and things to see than they knew what to do with and, given reasonable basic care, were thriving

Of course, the doctor didn't use the word "love" (words like that upset scientists) but he spelled it out clearly enough. What was important, he said, was:

+ skin-to-skin contact, frequently, and from two or three special people
+ movement of a gentle but robust kind, such as carrying around, bouncing on a knee, and so on
+ eye contact, smiling, and a colorful, lively environment
+ sounds such as singing, talking, goo-gooing, and so on

It was an important discovery, and the first time that it had been stated scientifically. Babies need human contact and affection (and not just to be fed, warmed, and cleaned). If they are not given these human ingredients, they may easily die.

So much for babies. But what about older children?

Here is an interesting thing—it's a graph of my estimate of the amount of touching (that's right, physical touching) that people receive as their lives unfold.

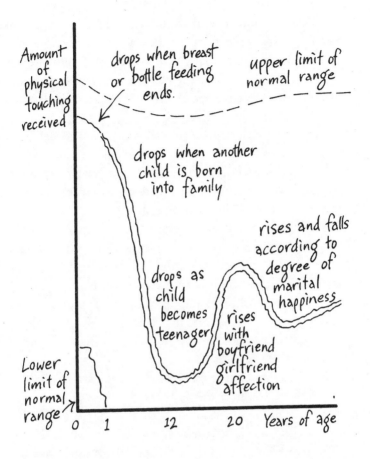

Remember, this is the average situation. Who knows what the ideal is—perhaps a line straight across. You may be wondering about the dip at about two to three years of age. That's when child number two (or three or four) usually comes along and affection has to be shared—a rough time for everyone.

Little babies like to be touched and cuddled. So do small children, although they are choosier about who does the cuddling. Teenagers often get awkward about it, but will admit in trust that they like affection as much as anyone. And, of course, by their late teens they are pursuing new sources of affection with great energy!

35

I once asked an audience of about sixty adults to close their eyes and then raise their hands if they got less affection than they would like to get in daily life. It was unanimous—every hand went up. After a minute the peeping began and the room began to ring with laughter. From this careful scientific study, I conclude that adults need affection, too.

Apart from physical touch, we find other ways to get good feelings from people. The most obvious one is by using words.

We all need to be recognized, noticed, and, preferably, given sincere praise. We want to be included in conversations, have our ideas listened to, and even admired.

A three-year-old says it out straight: "Look at me."

Most rich people take very little pleasure in their bank balance unless it can be displayed and someone is there to notice.

I often have a good chuckle to myself with the thought that most of the adult world is made up of big three-year-olds running about shouting, "Look at me, Daddy," "Watch me, you guys." Not me, of course—I give lectures and write books out of mature adult concern!

So, an interesting picture emerges. We take care of our children's bodily needs but, if this is all we do, they still miss out. They have psychological needs, too, and these are simple but essential. A child needs stimulation of a human kind. (It isn't enough to plonk her in front of a TV set.) She must have a diet of talking each day, with some affection and praise added in, in order to be happy. If this is given fully, and not begrudgingly from behind a pile of ironing or a newspaper, then it will not even take very long to accomplish.

Many people reading this will have older children, or teenagers. You may be thinking, "But already they have learned some bad ways of getting attention. How can I deal with that?"

Here is another story:

"Of Mice and Men"

A FEW YEARS ago, psychologists wore white coats and worked mostly with rats. (Nowadays they wear tweed jackets and work mostly with young women—things are looking up!) The "rat psychologists" were able to learn a lot about behavior because they could do things with rats that they couldn't with children. Read on, and you'll see what I mean.

In one particular experiment, rats were placed in a special cage, with food and drink, and a little lever. They ate, drank, and ran around, and eventually asked themselves the same question you are asking: "What's the little lever for?" They pressed it (being like children, they wanted to try everything) and, to their surprise, a little window opened in the cage to reveal a film being shown on the wall outside. Perhaps it was Mickey Mouse—I don't know! The window soon closed and the rat had to press the lever again to get more of the movie.

The rats were willing to work very hard at lever-pressing to keep the movie in view, leading us to principle one: intelligent creatures, such as rats (and children), like to have something interesting to do. This helps their brains to grow.

The researchers then put the rats in a different cage, with food and drink but no lever and no window. The rats were content for a little while but then started misbehaving. They chewed the walls, fought with each other, rubbed their fur off, and were generally bad rats. This leads us to principle two: intelligent creatures, such as rats (and children), will do anything to keep from being bored, including things we could call silly or destructive.

Finally, the researchers really got nasty. They tried a cage with food and drink, and with little wires placed across the floor and attached to a battery. Every now and then a shock was sent through the wires, enough to give the little creatures a real start but not to injure them. (You see now why they didn't use children.)

Finally, the exciting moment arrived. The rats were taken out of the cages and given a choice of which cage they would prefer to go back into. Perhaps you, the reader, could make a guess as to which was the rats' first choice, second choice, and so on. Here they are again:

+ cage with food, drink, and movies
+ cage with food and drink
+ cage with food, drink, and unexpected shocks

Have you guessed? Well, the rats preferred the movies best of all. If you didn't guess that one . . . back to the start of the book! The second choice was the really interesting one: they preferred the cage with shocks to the one with only food and drink. This leads us to principle three, an important principle indeed for children: intelligent creatures, like rats (and children), would rather have bad things happening than nothing at all.

✦

Or, in other words, any stimulation or excitement is better than none even if it's somewhat painful.

In child terms, if a child has to choose between being ignored and being scolded or even smacked, which do you think he'll prefer? Which do your children choose? Of course, if positive attention is available, at least once or twice a day, then neither of the above will be so appealing.

I'll conclude this section with one more story—this time about children. You are smarter than children or rats so it won't need any explaining!

*A*N UPWARDLY mobile young couple had two boys, ages nine and eleven. The boys had a playroom under the house with a billiard table, a refrigerator full of soft drinks, a TV, a record player (video games hadn't been invented at that stage, or they would have had one of those, too), and so on. However, the parents found that, despite the facilities provided, the boys were always fighting; it was even embarrassing to have guests for dinner. They finally took the boys to a behavioral clinic to seek the help of psychologists. The psychologists said to the parents, "Well, we mostly know about rats, but we're willing to come over and have a look." The arrangements were made. The parents thought it a little odd, but were keen to solve the problem that was badly affecting their social life.

The psychologists came in a team and installed themselves around the house with notepads and stopwatches. It was the evening of a cocktail party, so some of the psychologists stayed upstairs (where the adults were) and some were with the boys downstairs (sitting silently taking detailed notes). At about seven o'clock the upstairs observers noted the mother glancing downward and then across at her husband. Simultaneously, the observers downstairs had noted that the boys, having played with the various games and toys, had begun to fight. The fighting was rather unusual, though—it had more the look of a stage fight or a kind of a dance. The noise, however, was very fight-like!

The observers in the basement then saw the father appear on the stairs and, having been told by the psychologists to act normally (not an easy thing to do), begin to yell at the boys for being disruptive. The psychologists scribbled furiously: they had noticed a unique thing, something they had never seen in rats. The boys listened to their father shouting and looked suitably chastised, except for a small and curious twist about the mouth—an expression that has become famous. Psychologists call it "the Mona Lisa smile" . . .

Child psychologists now realize that this half-smile is a secret message, which means, "Well, I should be feeling bad, and I'm trying hard to look remorseful, but, you know, I'm kind of enjoying this!" Parents have never really figured this out but they react to it unknowingly with that famous parent sentence, "Wipe that smile off your face when I'm talking to you!"

Meanwhile, back in the basement, the boys were getting more attention from Dad than they had received all day and had to struggle hard not to show their pleasure.

The psychologists went back to their laboratory, prepared a detailed report, and met with the parents to tell them what you have probably already guessed: "You're too busy with your social life; the boys need more attention. They like their dad because boys of this age want to learn how to be a man, and so they have found the one thing that they know will bring their dad into the picture: fighting."

The psychologists were right, but they didn't understand the parents very well. The parents' reply was, "What a load of rubbish. How could children possibly like being told off?" The parents, you see, didn't know about the rats and the electric shocks, let alone the Mona Lisa smile.

The parents took their boys off to a psychiatrist, who analyzed their dreams for two years; then their dad gave up and took them golf-playing with him, which of course cured them!

There is a fourth reason children act up, and this is very much a symptom of modern life. Some children haven't learned the ability to be calm, or to self-soothe. How else can we explain the sudden worldwide epidemic of Attention Deficit Hyperactivity Disorder? The solution—prescribing mind-altering drugs—may be necessary for short-term management, but ADHD is not caused by an amphetimine deficit! If it were, it would be a vitamin R, and be put in cereals like all other vitamins! ADHD drugs activate parts of the brain that help calm it down, but they don't address the cause. No one knows the cause, but the most promising avenue is that we are simply too stressed and overstimulated in our lifestyles, and some children are vulnerable to this. Early indications are that if children, babies, and even pregnant parents have calmer environments, less or no TV, less noise, more physical activity of the vigorous kind followed by quiet times, and are taught meditation or similar self-control skills, they have the best chance of learning to be focused and successful without needing drugs. There are now numerous books on non-drug approaches to ADHD.

✦

We can easily summarize the above:

Children act up because they're bored.
Is there something you could do to give them more stimulation—go to the park with a ball, have their friends over, join a play group, have a box of odds and ends for imaginary play so that they, and you, don't feel "caged in"?
Children act up because they feel unwanted.
Can you spend a little time each day giving full, positive attention and physical contact? And are you relaxed and happy enough to give *them* a secure feeling?
Children play up because it gets them noticed.
Watch for the Mona Lisa smile, a sign that some attention is needed for doing the *right* thing.
Children act up because they are overstimulated and need help to calm down.

Talking Is Brain-Food
for Kids . . .

*B*Y THE time they reach school age, some kids can talk very well and have a wide vocabulary. Some on the other hand are very limited in their verbal skills. This can be a real disadvantage. For one thing, teachers often use talking skills as an indicator of intelligence and ability, so your kids can be either deliberately, or unconsciously, labeled as "slow."

How can you help your kids to be good with words? And why the differences?

It was found as early as the 1950s that parents fall into two distinct groups in their approaches to talking to children. Some people are very abrupt and brief in what they say to their kids:

"Dwayne, shut that door!"

"Get over here!"

"Eat it!" . . . and so on.

Others were the opposite:

"Charles sweetheart, would you mind closing the door—it's blowing a cold draft on little Sebastian. That's a good boy!"

You don't have to be a professor to see that young Charles is going to have more words in his head than little Dwayne, and more ways of stringing them together. (Though on the other hand Dwayne may also know some words that Charles doesn't!)

Most parents today talk to their children, explaining things and just chatting to them for the pleasure of it. Even babies enjoy being chatted to, and toddlers understand much more than they let on.

Here is how to give your child a language-rich environment:

1. DURING PREGNANCY, make lots of sounds to and around your baby. You can start by singing or crooning when you feel like it, or having music playing (even loudly is fine). If you're a dad, snuggle up and talk to your wife or even directly to the baby! This way your child will come to know and feel safe with your manly voice and be easier for you to comfort when he is little. Repetition and familiarity helps— the sound of TV's *Days of Our Lives* theme music has been found to soothe newborns who "listened" to it with Mom during pregnancy!

2. WITH AN INFANT, continue all this talking, singing, and music exposure once the baby is born. Moving or swinging him or dancing around will add to his delight and sense of rhythm, which is a necessary part of speech. (Special high-speed movies have been taken that show that we all do a subtle swaying dance as we speak—that it is almost impossible to be still while speaking.) If you can carry the babe around with you in a sling or harness as you work, all the better.

   As you go through the day with your toddler, tell him about what you are doing, using simple words, but not all baby talk. Use repetition of those words he says to you, so as to polish up what he is saying.

3. AS YOUR TODDLER STARTS TO TALK MORE, you can help by echoing and adding to what he says to you, so he is both encouraged by the response and helped to get the words right.

   "Buppa!"

"You want the butter?"

"Want buppa!"

And a little later:

"Pass butta ayy?"

"You want me to pass the butter?"

"Pass me butter!" . . . and so on!

Do all this casually, as a game, with no undue pressure or expectations.

A recent TV series featured interviews with "super-bright" or "hothouse" kids. It gave us some mixed feelings; these kids were certainly high achievers, but some by adulthood had turned into real oddballs! One family stood out, though, for the naturalness and balance of their kids. Their four daughters, ranging in age from eight to sixteen, were friendly, relaxed, very down-to-earth, and yet extraordinarily advanced in their skills. The sixteen-year-old, for instance, had simply skipped high school (at her teacher's suggestion—the parents had been quite happy for her to go). She was now doing doctoral research into spinal cell damage. Asked how they had raised such genius kids, the father said, "It couldn't be genetic—I haven't had the sperm bank knocking on my door!" (And he did look, well, rather ordinary!) The mother added that "We just explain to them . . ." She explained that as she vacuumed the house, for example, she would tell the baby she was carrying on her back about what she was doing, that the noise was made by the motor inside the vacuum cleaner, which was electrical and turned very fast, that the air it blew through made a lot of noise, and so on . . .

One could imagine her manner being cheerful and natural—not "schoolmarmish," giving stern lectures, but rather, "Hey, this is interesting!" If you find car trips or shopping with little children rather boring at times, then perhaps this kind of chatter will make it more fun for both of you.

In our family we found that this creates a whole new problem—how to stop a four-year-old from talking ALL THE TIME! But at least she does it well.

✦

Fathering—
Doing Things Together

*W*HEN OUR son was small we lived on a quiet country lane, half a mile from the post office and general store. It was a nice walk to get the mail, on a sunny morning, and took ten minutes there and back. Unless you took a two-year-old! Two-year-old kids do not think like adults—they do not know the meaning of "long-term goals." They don't even have "application to the task at hand." Anything but. Each step of the way has to be the subject of intense negotiations: "I wanna play inna green water!"

Once, out of dedication to science, I tried something out. I completely gave in, and let "the kid" investigate every drain, ditch, dead worm, puddle, and rock that he wanted to, along the way. (If early influences determine eventual careers, my son will be something big in sewage.) Anyhow, to cut a (very) long story short, it took two and a half hours! After a while, I even started to enjoy it!

It's very clear from everything we know about families, that kids—especially boys—get a lot out of being around fathers. Something different and complementary to what mothers provide takes place at these times. And for the most part, being with fathers means "doing things together." It's not like in all the movies and shows like *The Waltons.* In the Waltons family they sit down and have "heart-to-heart talks." Of the adults I spoke to, those who got along well with their dads did some talking and listening—but it was carefully concealed amid activity. Trust and self-disclosure grow gradually, while on the surface we are just loading the wood, working on the car, going to a ball game.

You'll notice some of these are rural pursuits. The city doesn't lend itself quite as much to doing things together—not so actively anyway. You can only take out the garbage so many times. City parents I talk to seem to get close to their kids while taxi-driving them between activities, from athletics to ballet and back to piano. This is the time to actually ask how they are doing and draw them out a little, though you have to time it to the trip.

For fathers, doing stuff with your kids is vital. It allows closeness to just happen. Conversations wander into deeper realms. Things just kind of pop out unguarded, and an relaxed but alert father can actually influence the direction of his own childrens' lives far better than leaving this all to Hollywood and peer groups.

When doing things with your children, some simple rules apply:

1. DON'T EXPECT TO ACTUALLY ACHIEVE ANYTHING! Especially with small children (as in going to the post office) the goal is no longer the goal. For example, if you are teaching them to use a screwdriver, you won't get the door hung in a great hurry. So let go of that one. They'll wander off in a while and you can make up for lost time.

2. ONLY DO THINGS WITH KIDS THAT YOU FEEL RELAXED ABOUT. Their help in planting out spring seedlings will not give you an immaculate garden. You have to decide which you are doing—being with your kids, or getting the job done to your usual standards. If you try to do both you will experience a little frustration. Settle for sweeping up some of the leaves, but mainly having fun together. That way they will see "gardening with Dad" as a fun activity, and ten years later will volunteer to mow the lawn!

3. ENJOY PARENTHOOD—IT DOESN'T LAST! I was in my thirties when my son arrived, and so am mindful of parenthood being all too short. If he wanders by when I'm doing a job, I value the contact with him and like to see what I can teach him there and then. But not when I'm writing on the computer!

In conclusion—as a father, you need to decide moment to moment what is more important to you, and it will sometimes be the kids, and sometimes not. One big plus is that kids tend to slow you down, and while slowed down, you start to rediscover little pleasures, which is the gift they bring. Time with kids is never wasted.

✦

~: three :~

Curing by Listening

HOW TO HELP CHILDREN
DEAL WITH AN UNKIND WORLD.

✦

Your CHILD IS upset. Something has gone wrong at school or with another child or the teacher, and you don't know how to help. You would like your child to find a way of dealing with the problem so he or she will be less vulnerable. This chapter will show you how to help.

The world is sometimes an unfair and difficult place for kids and, much as we would like to, we parents can't smooth out all the bumps. In fact, we shouldn't, since it's through dealing with difficult people and situations that our children become mature and independent adults.

We'll look first at what *not* to say to kids when life is treating them badly: the kinds of statements that can put a wall between you and your child. Then you'll learn of a remarkable skill called "active listening," which parents are finding is the most positive way they can help kids deal with life.

Since we are their "safe harbor," children often bring problems to us to see if we can help. The way that we react to these calls for help will either open up greater trust or put up a barrier that will be hard to take down. There are three ways that parents typically react that cause the barriers to go up:

Rescuing

"Oh, you poor thing. Here, let me fix it for you."

Lecturing

"Well, you are stupid to have got into this mess, so I'll tell you what to do. Now, listen carefully to me . . ."

Distracting

"Oh well, never mind, let's go and play catch."

Which is your style? Do you rush to the rescue, give wise advice, or change the subject?

Let's take a closer look at each of these three styles.

RESCUING

"How was your day?"
"Bad!"
"Oh, you poor thing. Come and tell me all about it."
"We had this new teacher for math. And I couldn't keep up."
"Well, that's really awful. Do you want me to help you with the work after dinner?"
"I didn't bring it home."
"Perhaps I could call the school tomorrow and talk to the principal?"
"Oh, well I dunno . . ."
"I think it's best to get to the bottom of things before it gets worse, don't you?"
Well, err . . . mmm."
"I wouldn't want your education to suffer."
"Uh-huh."

LECTURING

"How was your day?"
"Bad!"
"Well, you're a fine one to complain. I'd love to be able to spend my day learning, having a nice easy time."
"Well, we had a hard time. We've got this stupid new math teacher . . ."
"Now don't you go talking about your teachers in that tone. If you paid more attention you'd be better off. You think

you should have everything handed to you on a plate!'
"Hmmm."

DISTRACTING

"How was your day?"
"Bad!"
"Oh, come on, it wasn't that bad was it? Want a sandwich?"
"Thanks. I'm a bit worried about math . . ."
"Well. You're no Einstein, but neither are your mom or dad.
 You go and watch TV and don't let it get you down . . ."
"Uh-huh."

You'll notice in all three examples the same thing happens: the parent does all the talking; the conversation stops pretty quickly; and the child doesn't get to talk over the real problem. So the child's feelings get lost along the way; the parent "solves" the problem—or thinks he has; and the child says less and less.

Now look at a different approach . . .

ACTIVE LISTENING

"How was your day?"
"Bad!"
"You look really unhappy. What went wrong?"
"Aw, we've got a new teacher for math. He goes too fast."
"You're worried you won't be able to keep up?"
"Yes. I asked him to explain part of it and he said just to pay
 more attention."
"Hmmm . . . How did you feel about that?"
"Really bad—the other kids all laughed at me . . . but they're
 having trouble, too!"

"So you're angry that you got into trouble because you spoke up first?"

"Yes, I don't like getting shown up in front of everyone."

"What do you think you'll do?"

"I'm not sure, I suppose I could ask him again, when the class is over."

"You think that would work better?"

"Yes, then I wouldn't feel so embarrassed. And I think he's a bit nervous, too. Maybe that's why he rushes."

"You can understand it from his point of view?"

"Yeah, I guess he's just nervous of us."

"No wonder, teaching such smart kids like you!"

"Yeah!"

This, then, is active listening. In such cases parents are far from silent: they are interested, and show it by confirming their child's feelings and thoughts and by helping the child to think it through. Using this approach:

+ parents rarely give remedies or attempt to rescue ("I'll call the school")–unless this is clearly necessary
+ they rarely advise ("You should ask for help")–unless the child really needs information
+ they rarely distract the child from the problem ("Oh well, have a sandwich")–unless the child is a chronic whiner!

The skill of active listening takes some practice to acquire, and is taught in classes called "Parent Effectiveness Training" around the country. It is also explained in the book of the same name by Dr. Thomas Gordon (see *References*, p. 163).

Many parents have found active listening a great relief. They don't have to keep their child forever happy and they don't have to solve the child's problems for him. With active listening they can help the child while leaving the responsibility, and pleasure, of a solution to the child. The trick is to ask yourself, "Could my child benefit, in the long run, from solving this problem himself?" You can offer time, clarity, and understanding so that a problem can be turned into a learning experience.

Sometimes parents must intervene, as the following story illustrates.

A friend of mine has a nine-year-old son who broke his leg and needed to wear a cast for several weeks. When the plaster was removed he was naturally shaky on his feet for a while. A physical education teacher at the elementary school he attended had the class run around the track and my friend's son came in last, an embarrassment to him because he was a good runner. The teacher, without waiting for an explanation, made the boy run the track again, but this time in his underwear only and in front of the rest of the class.

When the boy arrived home in tears and his parents learned of what had happened they were so angry that they saw the school principal the same night and asked that the teacher be dismissed. The teacher was, in fact, transferred to another school, where we can only hope the same does not happen again.

This is a case in which parents must become involved and defend their children's rights because the children are powerless to defend themselves. In some cases, though, kids do NOT want our help—just our support. To get involved at these times would be the wrong thing . . .

"Just listening" is powerful medicine. If we can hold back from putting instant Band-Aids™ on every hurt, we can enter the deeper world of our children.

Mandy, age six, was in a bad mood. In fact, she had been out of sorts for a few weeks. She was acting mean toward her younger brother, whom she usually adored, and had started not wanting to go to kindergarten in the mornings. Her mother decided to use "active listening" to see if she could find the trouble. She asked Mandy, "You look sad. Do you want to tell me about it?" Mandy came and sat on her lap but didn't talk much.

Next day, Mandy had to be stopped from fighting with her baby brother and was put in her room for a few minutes to cool off. Later that night, Dad commented, "You seem kind of upset at the moment."

Mandy gave one piercing look at her mom and burst into tears. "They call me Yuk Face." In the next ten minutes or so Mandy moved through anger and tears in succession, while her mom resisted the urge to distract her or try to cheer her up. Mandy did indeed have a scar on her face, which one day would be healed with surgery, but for a while she would have to live with it.

When she had let out some of the bad feelings she'd collected from children at school, Mandy was much more peaceful. "I'm not yucky, am I, Mommy?" "Nope! You're terrific!"

Sometimes children want you to do something—in which case they should ask straight out.

Jonathan, age fourteen, hung around the kitchen for ages, looking very awkward. Finally he told Mom, with some embarrassment, that an older girl had asked him to go to a motel for the night with her! His mom had to battle hard not to start laying down the law. She said instead, "Gee, what do you think you'll do? You sound like you're feeling pretty unsure."

"Well, I don't know. Mom, would you forbid me to go? Please?"

Jonathan's mom was very happy to forbid him to go. Jonathan was most relieved: he saved face at school and with the girl. Jonathan's mother told me later that she would have forbidden him to go but wanted him to make his decision, too. A brave lady!

~ **four** ~
Kids and Emotions

WHAT IS REALLY GOING ON?

♦

This IS PROBABLY a good place to make a confession. The title of this book, *The Secret of Happy Children*, is a little idealistic! In the adult world, no one is ever, or would want to be, continually happy. So for our children such an aim actually would be wrong. If you try to make kids happy all the time, you will actually make them and yourself miserable! What we really want is kids who can handle and move along through the many feelings that life brings. Joy is the goal, but being comfortable and experiencing all the emotions life brings is the way to get there most often.

A proper understanding of emotions has been missing in our culture until recently. We've only just escaped from the era of "big boys don't cry," and "it's not ladylike to get angry." Few areas of understanding are as needed and helpful right now as getting back in touch with how feelings work. Luckily, the "facts about feelings" are now available to help both us and our kids to find the inner peace and vitality that make up emotional health.

WHAT DO WE MEAN BY EMOTIONS?

EMOTIONS ARE DISTINCTIVE sets of body sensations that we experience under specific situations. They range in intensity from subtle to incredibly strong. They are constantly with us—flowing and merging together as we resolve each event in our life and move on. *We are always feeling something*—emotions are a symptom of being alive!

There are four basic emotions—*anger, fear, sadness,* and *joy*. All other shades of feeling are a mix of these—like colors mixed from the primaries, red, yellow, and blue. There are thousands of combinations possible—such as jealousy, a mixture of anger and fear; or nostalgia, a mixture of joy and sadness. We are such interesting creatures!

When our children are newly born, their emotions are only just beginning to take shape. Observant parents can watch babies in the early months developing separate and distinct expressions of how they are feeling—the shriek of fear, the tears of sadness, red-faced rage, and chortles of joy.

Infants are not inhibited; they *express* feelings naturally and easily, and as a result the negative emotions soon pass. However, a growing child has to *learn* how to deal with feelings socially, and find constructive outlets for the powerful energy that feelings create. A child depends on us as parents for this information. Luckily, it isn't too hard to get this right, as we'll show.

WHY DO WE HAVE EMOTIONS?

SOMETIMES YOU COULD almost wish you had no feelings. Especially the negative ones, such as anger or sadness, which cause so much pain. Why then did nature equip us with these highly charged states? Each has a big role to play, as you'll see.

Take anger first. Imagine a person who for some reason never feels anger. Somehow he was raised without a cross bone in his body! Heis standing one day in the shopping center parking garage. A car drives up and parks right on his foot! Our super-accepting person would just stand there waiting until the driver did her shopping and came back!

Anger is what makes us stand up for ourselves. Without it we would be slaves, doormats, mice! Anger is our instinct for freedom and self-preservation.

Fear is of definite value too. Why else do you drive on the correct side of the road? Fear keeps you from taking big risks. If you don't believe fear is useful, recall the times when you've been the passenger in a car with a driver who seems to have no fear! Fear slows us down, forces us to stop, think, and avoid danger—even when our conscious brain has not yet fathomed what that danger might be.

Sadness is the emotion that helps us to grieve; it literally washes us clean of the distress of losing something or someone from our life. The chemical changes that go with sadness help our brain to release the pain, and so move on to new life. Only by being sad can we "let go" and make new contact with people and life.

So you can see that, properly handled:

+ *anger . . . keeps us free*
+ *fear . . . keeps us safe*
+ *sadness . . . keeps us in contact with people and the world*

All three of these outcomes are central to our happiness. Joy, the fourth emotion, is what we experience when these needs (freedom, safety, and contact) are fulfilled.

TEACHING KIDS ABOUT ANGER

YOU CAN TEACH your kids specifically how to understand and handle each of the three "negative" emotions. Let's take anger first.

The first impulse that children have when they are angry is to lash out. This has a natural purpose, but must be modified somewhat if we are to get along in the world.

Whenever we intervene with children, our aim should be to help them learn what will work and serve them well as adults. Think for a moment: What is an ideal way for an adult to handle anger? It comes down to a balance. A person who is being mistreated in some way needs to be able to say so out loud, with conviction, and to do so early on (before she feels or acts violently). Anger and violence are not the same thing. Violence is anger gone wrong.

An adult learns to moderate his anger so that it has impact but does not do damage or become abusive. If our child shows too little anger, she may be seen as a wimp, and be pushed around or used by other kids. Too much anger makes her unpopular or even a bully. Getting this balance right is what our kids need to learn about–and it takes a few years of practice, starting from toddler age on.

⌣ॱ   ॱ∽

Survey-Assessing Your
Child's "Emotional Literacy"

NAME OF CHILD _____

POSITION IN FAMILY _____

Able to express anger   ❑

0 not at all   **1** only by tantrums,   **2** strongly and able
                        acting out,   to say they are
                        aggression   angry, in words, safely

Able to express sadness   ❑

0 not at all   **1** only by   **2** able to say they
                        converting it to   are sad, cry, get
                        anger or sulking   a hug

Able to express fear   ❑

0 not at all   **1** only by lashing   **2** able to speak
                        out, attacking,   fears out loud,
                        or withdrawing   talk them over

Able to express happiness   ❑

0 not at all   **1** only by acting   **2** able to say
                        "stupid,"   they are happy,
                        thoughtless,   dance and sing,
                        or agitated   hug and laugh

If you'd like, you can add these up to give an emotional literacy score out of a possible score of 8. Six or below needs work!

✦

If you can see where your child is having trouble, you can encourage and help him to talk through what he is really feeling and why. Children can do drawings if they are young. Toddlers can point to the drawings of faces to tell you what they are feeling. This takes a lot of gentleness and care. Perhaps you too can work on expressing feelings and show your child by your own example how to be emotionally honest and expressive in safe ways.

To help kids be comfortable with anger:

1. Insist that they use words instead of actions to express anger. Get them to say out loud that they are angry, and, if possible, why.

2. Help them to connect their feelings with reasons. Talk with them to check out what is behind their outburst. Young kids will sometimes need help to "think back" to what went wrong:

   "Are you angry with Josh because he took your truck?"
   "Did you get sick of waiting for me to finish talking?"
   Soon they will be able to tell you what is wrong and why—instead of going straight to impulsive actions (like hitting Josh or kicking you in the leg!).

3. Let them know that feelings are heard, and accepted (but may not always change things).

   "You've got a right to be angry with me. I wasn't listening. I'm listening now."
   Or . . .
   "I know you're tired of waiting in this shop, and so am I, but that's just how it is. What can you do to pass the time instead of hassling your brother?"

4. Teach directly that hitting is not an acceptable way to handle anger. Confront this directly, give a negative consequence for each and every hitting instance, and insist that a child do what she should have done in the first place (usually USE WORDS)!

5. Help children to say what they DO want. Often they will start to whine and complain about what they don't want. They need your help to be more positive:

   "He hits me." "Tell him very loudly not to do that."
   "Myra took my bike." "Go and ask her if you can have it back now. Tell her politely it's yours and you want it."

6. Show them by your own example. When it's all added up, they are more likely to do what you DO than what you SAY. So be sure to role-model what you want. When YOU are angry, say so, in a loud voice. Get angry and be loud early, before you are REALLY steamed up. Once it is dealt with, let go, so they will learn that anger can be expressed, and then is gone. Simply say the words often and easily:

   + "I'm angry!"
   + "You're crowding me!"
   + "Stop interrupting!"

   "I'm annoyed that you didn't keep our deal. What's going on?"

Kids learn far better about anger from a parent who is moderately expressive than one who is always sweet, reasonable, and contained. Kids need to see that parents are human too.

You can be very angry with kids without ever being abusive, or using put-downs. Just stick to the direct expression of feelings and reasons. For kids, getting anger right takes a while. Be happy if your children are showing SOME signs of restraint; for example, if you see them holding back from hitting another child, or you, or you hear them saying out loud "I'm angry." Many adults haven't learned these lessons yet, so you are making good progress.

TEACHING KIDS ABOUT SADNESS

THERE HAS ALWAYS been a folklore understanding of sadness—that it's good to have a cry when things become too much. Fighting against this has been the notion of "being a man" or "being strong." Also in everyday usage among kids is the idea that you can cry too much, and that to do so is suspicious. There's even a special name for this, being a "crybaby."

To cry sometimes is as necessary and as natural as breathing. Far from making you strong, not crying actually makes you uptight; you tend to live in the past and be hard to contact in the present, and fearful of other people's emotions or anything associated with death or loss. If you know how to cry and release sadness, you know you can handle anything.

Scientists have found that when a person cries, his body releases chemicals of the endorphin family, which block pain receptors and produce a healing anesthesia through the worst of the anguish that loss sometimes brings. This chemical is present even in our tears themselves. It's closely related to, and as powerful as, morphine. If we held back our tears too much, we miss out on the healing power of this natural chemical.

To help kids be comfortable with sadness:

Sadness follows its own course as long as we provide support and understanding. All we need to do is be present and calm ourselves down as we sit or stand with a child who cries. Sometimes she will want to press against us and be held; other times she will want to be separate.

If it feels right, you can give permission: "It's okay to cry," "It's really sad about Grandpa," "I'm sad too." You can explain slightly if a child is confused or awkward: "Tony was a good friend of yours. He's worth feeling sad about."

We once were at a friend's place. We were watching a movie on video called *Mask* about a boy with deformities who dies in his teens. It had just ended, and everyone was enjoying being sad; in fact our hostess was sobbing loudly. Her three-year-old appeared at the door in pajamas, came over to Mom, put out a tender hand, and said "It's okay, let it all out!"

HELPING CHILDREN HANDLE FEAR

FEAR IS SOMETHING we all need. It's vitally important that children learn to freeze, and stop from running into danger. Also we want to know that they can run or jump quickly to avoid being hurt by a speeding car or a bicycle veering their way on the sidewalk going to school. And in our urban world, to fear the over-friendly stranger or a person acting strangely is also vital.

On the other hand, being too afraid is a real handicap—children need to be able to speak to adults, talk up at school and get their needs met, and join in socially. They need to see the world as a basically safe place, if handled properly. We'd like them to be brave enough to try new things—sports, new friendships, creativity, and so on.

Fear has two purposes. First it focuses you. A snake rearing up in front of you on a walk in the woods soon stops you from being dreamy and careless. Second, fear also energizes you. You will run faster and jump logs higher than you thought possible!

What kids need to learn in order to deal with fear is summed up in one word: THINK. We use our minds to sort out our fears, to plan for what we may need to do. When my job involved a lot of flying around the country, I found myself becoming more and more unhappy on planes. They felt unsafe—high up, bumping through clouds, wings flexing and so on. I had to think things through, such as the fact that no Australian jetliner had ever crashed, that plane travel is safer than road travel, that all around the world thousands of jets are routinely in the air all the time. And I found this worked. This is exactly the approach I take with kids.

Four basic hints for dealing with fears:

1. BE VERY MATTER-OF-FACT. Three- and four-year-old children often start to think more about the wide world around them, and come up with lots of concerns. This stage is even known as the "fearful fours" in some books. Talk it over with them. Be patient but casual. Trust their intuition; sometimes their caution about people or places will be well founded. Fear is a kind of radar, which has served the human race well through a dangerous past.

2. TALK FEARS OVER. If a child raises a realistic (if remote) fear, then explain the unlikelihood of it happening, but do figure out an action plan—discussing with him what he would need to do to feel safe again.

3. IF THEY RAISE AN UNREALISTIC FEAR, TELL THEM SO. Don't search under their bed for monsters, unless you live in the Komodo Islands or somesuch place!

4. UNDERLYING FEARS. If they are constantly fearful, use your listening skills to find out if there is something else that is troubling them that they find hard to tell you. Sometimes one fear is a cover for another that is harder to share.

In summary, kids need a little fear in their lives to protect them. They don't need overloading with adult fears—it's our job to take care of those. They need to be taught how to think through danger situations, and one good way is to plan with them: "What would you do if . . ." in response to questions they ask, or dangers you want to prepare them for.

RACKETS—WHEN FEELINGS GET OUT OF HAND

CHILDREN HAVE LOTS of real emotions, but sometimes we get the feeling that our child is "putting on" emotions, and this can be both puzzling and exasperating. For instance, some children always whine, while some are always angry and tantrumming, and others are always acting shy and afraid. If we can get to the bottom of these unhelpful patterns, then perhaps we can change them and make a huge difference in their way of relating to life. As parents, we tend to be suckers for a particular emotion that presses our buttons, probably due to some past experiences of our own that would warrant a whole segment on *Oprah*! Also, children are tempermentally different, and so many may need extra help to overcome being fearful, for example. If things are left to chance, children often get such a good reaction when they show a particular emotion that they learn to enact that feeling whenever they want the desired effect.

Feelings that are "faked" by a child in this way are called "racket feelings"

Anger when put on as a racket is called a *tantrum*.
Sadness when put on as a racket is called *sulking*.
Fear when put on as a racket is called *shyness*.

These three rackets comprise some of the major challenges to parents of young kids, so let's look at practical approaches to each.

Getting on Top of Tantrums!

*T*ANTRUMS ARE learned by accident. A child of eighteen months to two years is just making a twofold discovery. First, that she has a separate will of her own, but secondly that she can't always control the world and other people in it. This takes some getting used to. Controlling one's own will is a little like learning to ride a wild horse. A parent's role is to be understanding and helpful but not to give in. Early temper outbursts can be seen as a valuable chance to teach your child to handle life with more good humor and flexibility. Naturally this might take a year or two to achieve! Tantrums, especially when done in public, are the gold medal challenge of parenthood!

So here's what to do when a tantrum happens:

1   CALM YOURSELF—by noticing your breathing and letting it be deeper and slower. Notice your muscles too, and let them go looser if you can. Don't have a tantrum yourself!

2   HELP YOUR CHILD—by sitting or standing close to her, or even holding and comforting her if she will let you. (If she is thrashing around on the ground you might have to settle for just staying close and

72

waiting patiently!) Don't smack her or yell at her—this just pumps more emotion back into her to erupt at another time. By staying calm and present, you are letting her know you still love her and that the world isn't going to end just because she can't have what she wants.

(If it's a public place where you feel embarrassed or exposed, you might want to take her out of the store or off to a quiet corner. At a friend's, you might take her to another room to have a talk.)

3 DON'T GIVE IN—whatever happens don't give her what she wanted as a result of having a tantrum. If you do, she will still be doing it when she is nineteen!

4 TALK IT THROUGH—When she has calmed down, and especially if she is three or older, speak to her about how tantrums are not a good way to get what she wants. Discuss how else she could act in that situation—to take turns with the toy, to wait while you are on the phone and then you will play with her, and so on. (It's not so much what you say, but that you stay matter of fact and don't lose your temper or give in that helps the child learn to do the same.)

5 PREVENTION—Most tantrums and scenes occur when you are both getting overloaded. You will come to know the signs that your child is becoming tired, or hungry, or even unwell, and be willing to change your plans for that long shopping trip or visit to Grandma's. We all need to be able to say "Hang on, this is too much" and take a break. Overachieving adults can learn to be less "driven" once they become parents, because little children can't stand the stresses we might put ourselves under.

Some children just have preferences—they like to fasten their own seatbelt, or put the video in the machine themselves. Or they like a certain daily or bedtime routine and need to stick to it to feel secure. Take this as a sign that life really is a little too much for them, and they need a quieter and more even tempo to their life.

The aim is a good-humored and philosophical child who finds a way to be happy and meet his or her needs in cooperation with others. Surely a goal that is worth a bit of working on.

✦

Bean Bagging—
How to Stop the Sulks

*I*T'S DEFINITELY worth an Academy Award. He is sitting on the bean bag, in the middle of the living room. You can't miss him. He isn't hiding his anguish! He issues loud and heartrending sighs. You can't ignore him, so you ask, "What's the matter?" The answer is time honored—"Nothin." And that's only round one!

Sulking and whining are aimed at proving something—to get you to show by your efforts that you care. You prove you care by hovering and guessing,

"Is it the food?"

"Was it something someone said?"

"How are things at school?"

"Are you not feeling too good?"

"Nope, nuh, uh-uh . . ."

Eventually he allows you to give him some sort of special treatment, but even then he is not really right—

just mollified temporarily, nursing deep existential hurt until the next time! You wonder if you are somehow deeply inadequate as a father or mother.

Enough already! Sulking works best if parents feel guilty in the first place. Perhaps you woke one night in a daze when he was a baby, accidentally took off his clean diaper and put on a dirty one! Or you stuck him with the diaper pin and now he's got post-traumatic stress. Perhaps you work long hours and hardly see him. You might have to make changes, but this doesn't mean you should let a child manipulate you for ice cream and new toys.

If we give attention and love to a child who is sulking, he learns a simple equation—that love comes through being miserable. If you want to be cared for, just work up a negative attitude, and people will give you free attention. The problem with this is that it becomes a way of life. Sulkers make a career of misery!

If a child sulks around me, I let them know "I care about you. I'd like to help. Think about what you really want. I'll be in the kitchen." And I leave him. Usually he comes along and gets more direct, and then I'm happy to help. Sulking is boring when you don't have anyone to sulk at.

Here are four key beliefs for an anti-sulk campaign:

1. Everyone—child or adult—does know what he wants. He just needs to think about it until he is clear.
2. Children can learn to ask for what they want, direct-ly, in words.
3. People need very little: food, shelter, air, affection, exercise.
4. All the rest are wants. And you don't always get what you want!

Give your kids more attention and interest when they are being happy. Don't ignore them or leave them to be raised by the TV or video games—and only pay attention if there's a problem. By sharing happy experiences they will learn that joy is more fun than misery, and activity is the best way out of depression.

✦

The Myth of Shyness

*D*O YOU have a shy child in your family? Well, after you've read this, you may want to change that! You see, shyness is a myth. It's a trap that kids get caught in, and don't know how to get out of. And while shyness may be cute in a child, it is a real handicap in later life. For the truth is, shy people miss out.

So how do kids get to be shy, and how can we help them to be more outgoing? Shyness starts by a mixture of accident and conditioning. We are all caught unawares in social situations sometimes, and get tongue-tied. This happens to kids, too. I once saw a clown go up to a toddler at a show, bend down close, presumably to say hello, and the toddler was nearly scared out of her wits! Actor Robin Williams recounts taking a two-year-old to Disneyland and finding out from the child's perspective that good ol' Mickey looked like an eight-foot RAT!

Some children are naturally more reticent; it's as if their nervous system is so sensitive that the world is naturally overwhelming. So whether it's accidental or inbuilt, children need our help to overcome shyness enough to have a happy life. After all, the people you introduce your kids to shouldn't be either dangerous or scary—so there's no need to act as if they are.

Here are the steps:

1. TEACH YOUR CHILDREN HOW TO BE SOCIABLE. This is very simple. When someone speaks to your child, or says hello, and you are around, explain to them that they should:

   ✦ look up at the person who has spoken to them
   ✦ say hello and add the person's name

   You can introduce people, saying "This is Peter (or Doctor Brown, or whoever), say hello to him, please!" The child looks up and says "Hello Peter," and that's it! For kids under four, leave it at that. They should not be the center of attention for more than a moment or two, or they will be pressured into being little performers. Saying hello and making eye contact is a good start.

2. INSIST THAT THEY DO IT! Three-year-old Angela was considered by her parents to be very shy. They often had guests visiting, and although Angela was boisterous and talkative at other times, she would become coy, hide behind her mother's skirts, and generally be awkward when new people were around. This behavior was extended to her meetings with other children.

   Her parents talked to us and decided on a course of action. They gave her clear instructions about how to look up and speak when spoken to. When a friend, who had often been before, came to visit, and Angie acted shy instead of saying hello, they told her to go and stand and think until she was ready to get it right. (Stand and think is a technique used by many parents now to help kids think a problem through—an alternative to slaps or yelling.) Angie stood by the wall, but made a fuss and was taken to her room. (By this time her parents were glad it was an old friend they had visiting, and not some judgmental stranger.) It usually takes effort to break through a pattern the first time. When Angie quieted down, she was brought back to the room. She immediately said "I'm ready." (She may be stubborn, but not stupid.) She then came out, easy as pie, and said "Hello, Maggie" to the visitor, and ran off and played happily. Soon afterward, she approached Maggie easily and showed her a toy and chatted. The problem hardly ever occurred again, and when it did a few seconds to stand and think solved it. Angela went from being a shy child to an outgoing one in a matter of days.

The only reason shyness persists in the first place is that some adults give so much attention to it. They think it is cute, lovable, and endearing, and make a great show of "drawing a child out." The child gets more attention than she ever would for just being straightforward.

The only times when kids should be scared of people are when you are not around, or when there is something amiss, e.g. an adult who is actually dangerous, drunk, or known or intuited by the child to be a sexual danger. These people should not be around your children in the first place. Watch out for extreme reactions in your kids, and as soon as possible find out the reason.

Outgoingness is really just a matter of getting started with people, being friendly, and making a move—after that things flow easily. By teaching your child to say hello, to make eye contact, and to introduce herself, she will make friends, enjoy people, and her skills will grow. She will have a more successful life in all sorts of ways—socially, at school, and in her career. It's well worth breaking the pattern early on.

✦

⁖ **five** ⁀

The Assertive Parent

FIRMNESS. DO IT—NOW.

◆

In MY EARLY work with families, I was always having my eyes opened in one way or another. One of the first big surprises was discovering that some of the most stable and happy children were being brought up by incredibly firm (to my way of thinking) parents. The secret seemed to be that these parents were hard but reliable—so consistent that their children knew exactly what the rules were and how to stay out of trouble. Because of this, they received punishment very rarely.

Most importantly, these children knew that they were expressly and unmistakably loved and valued unconditionally. Rejection was never a possibility. These kids would have sometimes been afraid, but never terrified and never made to feel abandoned. In brief, there were strong rules plus positive affection. If there had been one without the other I don't think it would have succeeded.

In contrast to these firm-but-fair families, I saw far more children who had lots of "freedom," and got away with terrible misbehavior, but were still miserable. Paradoxically these kids were often from progressive or alternative families, and at other times had very indulgent and well-off parents. Clearly, these children were looking for someone to put the brakes on them, and their parents misunderstood the signals. They thought the children wanted more room and more freedom, but the opposite was true.

Children's need for limits is one of the secrets that parents need to know about. When social workers place a child in a foster home, after that child's own home has disintegrated, they have learned to warn the foster parents:

"This child may settle in easily but, more probably, he will act up a great deal in the first three months to test out you and your family unit–to see if it is strong enough to hold him. He will want to know if your marriage, your mental health, your affection, and your discipline are strong enough. *Then* he can relax and begin to grow again. In short, he wants to know that this family will not break like the old one, and will test it to see!"

Fostering is the extreme example. But all children are the same: they need to know that someone is going to stop them.

We know from research that there are three main styles of parental response to children's acting up: aggressive, passive, and assertive. Aggressive parents use attack, either in words or action, to put their children down. Passive parents allow children to "walk all over" them and only regain control when it's "the last straw"–and then by unexpected outbursts. Assertive parents are quite different from either of the above. Let me explain the three to you in more detail.

THE AGGRESSIVE PARENT

AGGRESSIVE PARENTS ARE angry with their children nearly all the time. Usually their anger is not a result of the child's behavior at all. They may perhaps be resenting their marriage, their job, the human race, or the fact that they're parents and don't want to be (which is no fault of the children). They let out this tension by putting the children down.

Some children deal with this in a very interesting way. They realize that this is a kind of love, reasoning thus: "At least they're interested enough to yell at me, and they yell loudly so they must care a lot!" The child may even yell back (to return the love), and soon parents and children are relating by fighting—kind of a "Bratty Bunch!" Whole families can join in. What to an outsider looks like a dangerous free-for-all is actually a kind of intimacy that all the participants would miss if it weren't going on!

Other children, sensing that parental put-downs are really destructive in intent, become withdrawn and disturbed.

As far as obedience is concerned, aggressive parents do get results, based on fear. However, they also get rebellion: many a bullying parent has one day faced a teenager big enough to hit back. Aggressive parents end up with children who are either frightened and intimidated or rebellious and defiant—or a mixture of both!

THE PASSIVE PARENT

PASSIVE PARENTS ARE everywhere!

I once interviewed a young mother who complained about her child's disobedience. This was quite a common complaint but there were one or two unusual things that caught my notice. Most parents bring the child with them to see me. In fact, many would like to drop them off, saying, "Here, you fix her!" This mother had not brought the child "for fear of upsetting her (and had not told her husband either).

As we talked, she poured out details of the child's behavior, obviously relieving herself of enormous worry and tension by putting it into words. She seemed so keen to unburden herself that it was a good half hour before I needed to speak. I asked how she dealt with disobedience and she replied that she was very firm but the child simply did not obey. I asked her to bring the child next time and show me.

The child was very helpful and lived up to our expectations. After a few minutes "casing the joint," she set about dismantling my telephone and curtains. I asked the mother to show me how she would stop the child. She immediately dropped her voice and murmured in soft, cautious tones, "Melissa darling, how about stopping that?"

Naturally, there was no change. "Please, honey, come here, there's a good girl."

I liked this lady: she was an involved parent and wanted to do what was best for her child. However, her idea of firmness was very unusual.

Some "assertiveness training" was tried, and some help to trace and change the causes of her timidity: Melissa soon ceased to wield the power in the family!

Good behavior in children is required not just to please the ego of the parents but to make practical living easier. Unlike parents of past generations, we do not need pointless obedience, such as brushing one's hair before sitting down for dinner or eating one's food in alphabetical order. We ask kids to cooperate so as to make life go more smoothly: "Put on your old clothes before you go out and play," or "Get that cat out of the fridge!"

Therefore, when a child does not cooperate, the parents find their life inconvenienced. Soft parents soon find they are being given the runaround. However much they want to give in and not inhibit little Sebastian's creativity, these parents find they are very angry and tired of the troubles this causes, and attempt to restore order. It may be after an hour of disobedience or a long rainy weekend of repeated trouble, but whenever it happens, the parents' patience suddenly runs out. They suddenly lash out and discipline the child in a way, and with a feeling, that they and the child know is somewhat out of control.

It will come as no surprise to you that parents who injure children are very often shy, timid parents who finally blow their stack. If you ever feel that you are a danger to your child's safety or your own when you "blow up," then be sure to read Chapter 8 of this book to find out more about self-care.

As I write this, I'm feeling a lot of concern that you, the reader, may be feeling bad, recognizing yourself in some of the above. If you have this pattern in your relationship with your child (back down, back down, back down, blow up), then you need to know a couple of things.

+ About a third of parents experience this pattern, especially when they have young children, and are just beginning to gain experience in parenting.
+ It is not a big problem, just a misdirection of your energies, and can be remedied.

So if aggressive and passive parenting don't work, what's left? Finally (with a trumpet fanfare!) we announce the ASSERTIVE PARENT.

THE ASSERTIVE PARENT

ASSERTIVE PARENTS ARE clear, firm, determined, and, on the inside, fairly confident and relaxed. Their children learn that what Mom or Dad says goes but, at the same time, that they will not be treated with put-downs or humiliation.

Assertiveness is not something you see every day and so you may not have a lot of examples to copy from. If your parents were aggressive, then it may be particularly hard for you to be assertive. The important thing is to see assertiveness as a skill, not something that you are born with. This means that you may take time to learn it. There's still hope!

The first part of assertiveness is on the inside of you, in your attitudes. Circle which is closer to describing you.

"Mush" parents devalue themselves	"Firm" parents decide they matter too
✦ I come last in the family.	✦ I'm as important as the rest of the family.
✦ I have to keep the kids happy all the time or I'm a bad parent.	✦ The children are important, but they have to fit in with others, too.
✦ I mustn't frustrate their natural creativity.	✦ Frustration is part of growing up: the kids can't always get their way.
✦ I'm nobody, really, but my kids might be someone someday.	✦ I need to be happy and healthy to be a good parent – I have to do things for myself, too.
✦ My spouse matters but not as much as the kids.	✦ My partner and our marriage are very important. The kids come an equal first.
✦ Life is such a struggle.	✦ Life is challenging but fun.
✦ I just want to keep the peace: I give in to the kids for the sake of some peace and quiet. Pity it doesn't last long.	✦ Life is easier if kids learn to behave well. As an adult I am the one in charge.

The second part of assertiveness lies in action: what you actually do. Here is how to get good behavior from a child who is used to disobeying or delaying.

1. *Be clear in your own mind.* What you're asking of your child is not a request, it's not open to debate: it's a demand that you have a right to make, and the child will benefit from learning to carry it out.

2. *Make good contact.* Stop what you are doing, go up close to the child, and get him to look at you. Don't give the instruction until he looks at you.

3. *Be clear.* Say, "I want you to . . . now. Do you understand?" Make sure you get a "yes" or "no" answer.

4. *If she does not obey, repeat what you want from her.* Do not discuss, reason, or get angry or scared. Breathe slowly and deeply so that you become calmer. What you are signaling to the child is that you are willing to persist on this one and not even get upset about it. This is the key step, and what matters most is what you don't do. You don't enter into debate or argument, you don't get heated, you simply repeat the demand to the child.

5. *Stay close* if there is any chance that the child will not carry out the task fully. When the task is completed (say, putting away toys), then don't make much of this either. Simply say, "Good," and smile briefly!

This sequence is a *retraining procedure*. It may well be time-consuming the first couple of times, so that you'll think, "Boy, it's easier for me to put the toys away!" But the time invested here will be repaid a thousandfold.

The trick is simply to persist. When the child discovers that you do not give up, have an entertaining minor nervous breakdown, or get sidetracked, then he simply gives in.

You will find that you soon develop a tone of voice and a posture that says "I mean business" to your child. It's completely different from the voice that you use to discuss, tease, praise, or play with your child. The child will recognize it as the voice that means "Do it now!" And they do! It's a great feeling!

Once they've grown accustomed to assertive parenting, it's amazing to look back at how you used to make things hard for yourself. For example, here is the Great American Bedtime Drama. Names have been changed to protect the innocent!

It's right around Cheryl's bedtime.

Mom	Child (to herself)
It's nearly bedtime, Cheryl. Better start packing up!	She said "nearly" – that means "not yet".
Are you packing up your toys?	Some chance!
You know how tired you get in the mornings, dear . . .	Mom's using reasoning with me – that means she's scared of me. Anyhow, morning is years away still.
Come on, Cheryl, you don't want to cause another fuss, do you?	Yep.
Look, I'll help you put the dolls away.	Goody! Mommy's gonna play with me!
Hey, put those toys back. I just packed them away.	Catch me!
Cheryl, do you want me to get really angry?	Yes! It's exciting.
You're a naughty, naughty child.	I guess I am. I don't know why, but I really enjoy these fights. They really get Mom involved.

The child's answers are, of course, unspoken. If Mom heard them she might not have been so willing to play along. The same sequence occurs in many situations. The main steps are:

+ the parents fear conflict: they sound reluctant and doubtful when they first "ask" the child to cooperate
+ they use reasoning and argument, not seeing that this is being used by the child to "buy time"
+ they give a lot of attention to struggling with the child, who enjoys the control and interest of having a big person on a string
+ the parents become fed up and respond with more emotion and put-downs than they really wanted to use

It's painful, especially if it happens every day. Thank goodness there's a way out.

One Way to be Angry and Relaxed at the Same Time— PRETEND!

ONE DAY when I was at school, our science teacher was called out of the room. Soon we had out the squeeze bottles of distilled water and were reenacting the gunfight at the OK Corral from behind the desks.

Although normally a timid child, I had seen every episode of *Gunsmoke* ever made. I got myself out to the front of the lab and was blazing away at the others, when suddenly their faces changed and they went still. A roar came from behind me and the teacher was back among us in a fury!

I was back in my desk almost by magic and didn't dare to even look up from my book. When I did, an amazing thing met my eye. The teacher was looking out over the silent class, grinning from ear to ear. I realized that he had been acting angry and was amused by the instant results he had achieved as a result.

This was new to me. I knew adults who got angry and went out of control, and others who got scared of their own anger, so that it came out all uneven. I decided that I liked this new kind better but that I'd stay in my seat in the future.

✦

We've explained discipline methods in more detail in *More Secrets of Happy Children.* If you're having serious problems with older kids—drugs, crime, etc.—a superb book called *Tough Love* gives very practical help plus describes parent support networks across the country (see *References* on p. 163).

The whole human race has been working out the discipline question for the last thirty or forty years, so you're not alone. Until this century, children weren't much of a problem: half of them died before adulthood; the remainder were seen as of little consequence unless they got to their teens and then they were classified as adults. Violence was the standard means of control. These were the days when seven-year-olds were sent down unventilated mines or stood at factory machines for ten-hour days. Childhood is looking up.

In the fifties and sixties came the great era of letting children be special. Like all new movements, the pendulum swung a little too far, so that youngsters found themselves with the troublesome burden of being the most important person in the whole family. Needless to say, this wasn't very good for them either. Finally, the pendulum is settling in the middle. We are learning to give both soft love and tough love, and our kids are starting to calm down.

So, that's the story on assertive parenting. It starts with the decision that you as a parent have rights, and that your child *needs* your control (even though he or she may not agree). It ends with a much happier life for everyone, with a lot more time for fun.

is not threatened
by conflict

negotiates more as
children become older
and more capable

ASSERTIVE

gives "positive strokes"

makes clear, firm
requests and demands

sets rules and carries
out the consequences

MANIPULATIVE

uses guilt, sickness,
etc. to get child to
behave

compares child with
others, etc.

**YOUR
CHOICE**

AGGRESSIVE

uses put-downs
to make children behave

shouts at children

hits child angrily

withdraws totally

gives in to all
child's demands

allows child to
misbehave

PASSIVE

Here are the four basic
choices mothers and
fathers have in dealing
with children – don't
use this chart to feel
guilty about your
behavior!

Use it to remind your-
self – "I have a
choice!"

Fathering—
Backing Up Your Partner

*M*ANY THINGS in life are more easily done with someone else's help, and one of those things is raising kids.

There's no doubt that, when handling kids, it takes energy, grit, and purpose in order to keep things running smoothly. Nothing feels better at these times than knowing you have the backup of your spouse.

Many progressive young mothers shy away from backup for a time, because they wanted to avoid the OLD WAY of doing things. What was the OLD WAY? It can be summed up in one sentence—"Wait till your father gets home!" This was not a fun arrangement—Mom, alone and overwhelmed, drops the disciplinary role onto Dad, who, when he gets home, just wants to relax but ends up being the bad guy to the kids, who then get away with murder with Mom when he's gone again, and so on.

Backup is important, but it has to be done properly. There is one simple rule: when you back someone up, you don't need to take over.

Relationships are simpler if people deal with each other directly. Whenever communication becomes three-handed, it gets confused. Here is an example of how to stay straight . . .

Peter, age thirteen, is hassling with Marjorie, his mom, about doing his share of the laundry. He gets louder and begins to swear, and is talking too aggressively. His father overhears this and walks in. He tells Peter, "Hey! You need to use a normal voice and sort this out with your mother now." He catches Peter's eye. "Right?" "Mmm." This sends a message that in this family, the adults are a team. The mother does not have to feel intimidated in her own home. She and her partner together insist that there be respect.

The principle is this: a child who is dealing with his mother over something has to complete that process with Mom. Where a father comes in is to ensure that the child is respectful and gets on with it. In this way everything is kept simple.

The need for backup can occur when dealing with both girls and boys. However, boys especially seem at certain ages to go in for concerted limit testing—and it's handy to have Dad to "bring on the cavalry." But backing up should be available both ways. Both parents have to strike a balance of firmness and kindness too. You can't "make up for" another parent's hardness or softness— each has to be a rounded person to the child.

Another OLD WAY that seems to have been incredibly common thirty years ago was the hard parent/soft parent combination—when one parent tried to make up for the other's harshness. Dad sends you to bed with no dinner, but Mom sneaks in with a snack. Or vice versa. This doesn't work too well, since the child doesn't experience either parent being balanced. If you are uncomfortable with your partner's parenting, talk it over privately with them—don't do it in front of the children.

As with everything else in parenting, you'll find a way that suits you. You'll know you're getting it right when your child says "That's not fair! You're both against me!"—but doesn't seem too upset about it most of the time!

✦

Kids and Housework—
How to Teach Responsibility

*H*ERE IS a neat way to reduce the housework you have to do, and help your kids get ready for adult life,—both at the same time!

In America kids have it very easy. We are often amazed to hear of young adults—in their twenties—living at home, being cooked for and having their laundry done by their aging parents. A lot of American kids don't grow up (that is, don't take responsibility for their own care and feeding) until they are in their early twenties. This is especially true of young men. Perhaps you are married to one!

All around the world, from Nepal to New Guinea to Nicaragua, it's normal for young children to have responsibilities. They are usually under watchful adult care but they have a daily round of chores that they carry out quite cheerfully and with obvious pride. There is also time for play, of course. The result of this working childhood is that in almost every other culture of the world, childhood flows smoothly and easily into adult life. How did we ever get the idea that childhood is a "waiting room" before real life begins?

Can we do a better job of helping our kids get ready for self-sufficiency in adulthood? Of course—and one way is by giving them work to do. You can start very early, from two years, when kids can have a small daily task, such as putting out the cutlery for dinner.

The tasks increase month by month. Choose tasks that are regular and easy, that involve self-care, and that contribute to the overall family welfare. By four they could set the table, as well as take their dishes to the sink. As they get older you will easily be able to think of tasks that you can add on. Remind them, and follow up on them, and in time simply expect them to remember. Give praise and be proud of them, but don't go overboard—this is no big deal, just what is expected.

Much is made these days of self-esteem and the importance of praising and valuing kids and their efforts. It's more important to remember that real self-esteem comes from contributing. Without knowing their place, and having a contribution, kids may get a kind of "movie star" self-image—a ballooned idea of themselves which the big world away from a doting Mom and Dad will be sure to deflate.

✦

This casual, graduated approach makes later stages much easier. Teenagers who have been helping out for as long as they can remember will not be resistant to pulling their weight—it will simply be routine. You're aiming for a young person who by the age of eighteen is doing as much work around the house as either parent. Cooking at least one family meal per week, as well as being responsible for some other area of family care. If sharing tasks between children, give them a mixture of the ones they like, and enjoy, and ones that are less pleasant. Again you are aiming to be realistic—just as in adult life.

What about study? Some adjustment may have to be made at times of exam pressure. But by and large, study and homework are simply their "day jobs," and shouldn't prevent them from making a contribution at home.

Remember, you are aiming for competence in all the basic areas of life—cooking, cleaning, laundry, care of animals, budgeting, time-management, as well as negotiation and teamwork. When your youngsters leave home, they'll do so fully equipped to look after themselves. In fact they'll probably leave sooner to escape all the work!

~ **six** ~

Family Shape

DAD? WHO'S DAD?

◆

What COMES INTO your mind when you hear the word, "family?" Older people would conjure up a gathering of thirty or forty people—aunts, uncles, cousins, and others—relatives who very likely lived in the same area and got together many times a year, if not weekly for Sunday dinner.

What we call families today are not families at all. We haven't had real families since the car was invented, and we became dispersed across the country or the world. The "two-parent, three kids, and golden retriever" family is only a piece of family, and that's why it doesn't work very well.

What's more, the picture above is changing, too. The average American family is now often either a single-parent family or a recombined family with only one of the child's parents and a new dad or mom, probably with their kids. This isn't necessarily a bad thing, but it is making life very different.

How does all this affect your children? Well, we have discovered that the shape of your family is very important, and you can alter its shape to make it a good place to be.

So read on!

Here then is the Steve Biddulph plan for government policy-making on families!

Let's use an example. Some people blamed all social ills on family breakdown:

"Where are you off to, Merv?"

"Just off with the guys to steal a car, Mom!"

"Well, don't be home late!"

Superficially, this is true, but what caused the families to break down? Have you ever seen the places where street gangs grow up? Or living conditions in Belfast or Soweto?

Income levels are important to start with. Below certain standards of "liveability," no one can raise happy children. Above a certain point, though, the need changes from material to human resources. Education, the development of community, and ways to belong and participate and work together with others emerge as the strongest needs for healthy family life.

This, in dollar terms, is very cheap. A friend of mine organizes self-help groups for people who've had breakdowns. If he keeps two people per year out of the hospital, he pays for his own salary. In fact, he achieves much more than that.

For thousands of years people lived in villages or small towns. When modern cities began to appear, about two hundred years ago, people still lived pretty much in the same neighborhood as all their relatives.

As you can imagine, it's quite a gathering of people. And although times were hard, with people dying in wars and a lot of deaths in childbirth or infancy, this extended family unit was very supportive. For example:

- Mary (who stayed single) loves kids, and so often has little Jenny to stay with her.
- This is good for Doris, with the three boys. Doris is often unwell and Mary cooks and helps clean once or twice a week.
- Ellen's husband, Len, died in the war. Andrew was born in 1920, which could have caused a few problems, considering the war ended in 1918, but, since Ellen moved in with Will and Naomi, no one outside the family needed to know!
- Grandpa is a little over the hill and keeps waking up thinking the Indians are coming but, luckily, Brandon, the youngest son, is living at home and looking after the farm.
- Wilfred doesn't like children and is often away, but Arthur likes children and so takes the boys fishing, playing catch, and so on—so they don't miss out too badly.

The twenty-four people in this hypothetical family don't actually live together (there are six households in all) but it would be a rare week that they didn't all see each other at some time or other. The family unit was able to withstand wars, illnesses, deaths, Ellen's "flying Scotsman," and various failings and foibles; and everyone belonged and was cared for.

It was a hard time, but there was less uncertainty. For parents, this had definite advantages. Right was right and wrong was wrong. If you weren't everything your children needed, there were others to step in. You were never alone—there was plenty of advice, help, and example. You got lots of practice with other people's children and your younger brothers and sisters before you started on your own. You could even choose not to have kids at all and still not be too lonely.

There were lots of restrictions and demands, too, and not many of us would go back, even if we could, to that kind of extended family. But the good things that were there for parents—

can we ever get those back? I think so, and would like to tell you how.

You Don't Have to Be Related—Just Committed

LET'S TAKE THE loneliest modern family: the single parent with one or two young children. (Some would argue that there is an even lonelier combination: the unhappily married family, the reason so many people go back to being single.) What is missing?

+ The grandparents may not live close by: we move about so much these days.
+ There may not be other adults who are interested in the kids—the uncles and aunts.
+ There may be no father figure to play with and be a back-up in discipline and decision-making (if you're a single mom).
+ There may be no woman to handle "girl's stuff," go to the school during the day to see teachers, or share in discipline and decision-making (if you're a single dad).
+ There may not be other kids to play with or safe places outside the house or apartment for the kids to go.
+ When really hard things happen there's no one to talk to that you can really trust or who will help you materially, just because you're "family."

But the fact that all of these things are not available doesn't mean that they may not be found. For instance, some old people really like kids. Might it be possible to find some "grandparents" who live nearby who could become part of your family? (You paint their ceiling, they mind your kids!)

There are other single parents, or not-single parents, dying of loneliness very close to you. Do you think people really go to

Tupperware parties to buy plastic bowls? They go for something to do, and someone to talk to. Other parents are dying to talk to you.

You can find out about groups that have been started in the community. Play groups are really just like Sunday afternoon at Grandma's house, where kids can play and parents can talk and join in. Courses run by adult education centers are good meeting places and very friendly. Schools, kindergartens, infant health centers, environmental groups, gym's, churches—choose whatever suits your style.

It's very hard work, and if you move you have to start all over again. Nonetheless, you can actually make yourself an extended family, if not for your own sake, then for your children's.

There's another part of family shape that is very important, even if your family is the official two adults and two-and-a-half kids. When you started out as a couple it was simple. There were just the two of you, and you probably had a good time. Then, when kids were added in, it might have started to get complicated. Many families find themselves caught in one of these "shapes":

You've probably experienced all three at some time. And with more kids, the combinations can get even tougher:

These are natural alignments for the family from time to time, but they are bad news if they become the normal shape of your family.

What we have found in hundreds of families seeking help is that *the closeness of the parent-couple is very important.* Kids seem to grow up most easily and happily when Mom and Dad are affectionate and interested in each other—to such a degree that the children could not come between them, even if they tried (which they do!).

One expert became famous for saying that the best sex education in the world was for Dad to give Mom a squeeze as he walked past her in the kitchen, and for Mom to obviously enjoy it! In the interests of non-sexism, I'm sure it would be just as good the other way around (Mom squeezing Dad!).

Kids actually seem to gain reassurance from the fact that parents spend time together and they are not allowed to interrupt. If you haven't been in the habit of doing this (so that the kids take precedence even when you are talking to your partner), then you should make an effort to break the pattern.

Problems seem to arise whenever:

+ a parent frequently sides with a child against the other parent
+ a parent seeks affection and approval from a child, in preference to, or instead of, his or her spouse
+ a child is forced into a parent role too often, for example, having to care for other children or being part of decisions that are really parents' decisions

Once at a funeral I heard a well-meaning relative tell a nine-year-old boy whose father had just died that he would have to "be a man now and take care of your mother." This is too much responsibility to put on a child.

Guidelines for keeping your family in shape.

Every family is different and no advice can be completely right. All I can do is give you the general rules that we have found, and which may apply to you and your children.

+ In a single-parent family, kids are happier when their parent has a close, affectionate relationship with another adult. Whether it is their natural parent or not, or whether the other adult is of the opposite sex or not, doesn't matter greatly; what matters is that their parent is happily supported by at least one special "other" adult.
+ Children suffer if conflict is ongoing, but they also suffer in marriage breakups. The research is very clear on this. Couples owe it to themselves to get good counseling and help to work on their difficulties. All marriages have tough patches–don't panic or give up too easily. Many difficulties in marriage are "portable"–you will encounter

them whoever you are married to. Unless your partner is violent, addicted, chronically dishonest, or totally refuses to communicate, your chances of improving things are very good. But it takes work.

A couple recently appeared in the family court to obtain a divorce. The man was ninety-one and his wife eighty-six. The judge, shocked at their old age, asked why they were getting divorced after all these years. They replied, as many couples before had, "We can't stand each other!"

"But why did you stay together all these years?" asked the judge in dismay.

"Because," said the couple, "we wanted to wait until the children had died."

But What If You're a Single Mom?

SINGLE PARENTHOOD has both advantages and disadvantages. The advantages are that you don't have to put up with differing standards, conflicts between parents, and so on. You're the boss! Separated mothers have often told us that life is a lot smoother. On the other hand, many things, such as discipline, are harder to do by yourself. Let's look at this.

Sometimes as kids are growing up, it's necessary to "lean on" them with a lot of strength and persistence. You can see the need to bring them into line, for your sake and theirs, but it just gets tiring. At certain ages boys especially are hard for single mothers to manage. It seems to be a biological need for some boy children to experience strong conflict, and be firmly and frequently controlled until they learn to temper their strength and rebellion and so get along with other people. Put simply, they actually seem to want a fight, and only relax and let up when you give it to them. At times like these, a father would come in handy.

One of the hardest things about being an only parent is that you want to keep a loving and accepting bond with your children, but also be able to discipline them. If you are their only source of support, then every dicipline time is scarier for you both because they may feel their only channel of love is endangered. With two parents, a child can hate you one day and your partner the next!

Especially with a teenager, an only parent sometimes has to step back from the brink of a fight by saying, "We are both too upset right now. Let's take some time to cool off and come back to it later." By being honest with a teenager that "we have to get along," it's possible to reach an agreement that there will not be abuse or dis-respect, and that basic cooperation will happen, so that the family can stay together and working for everyone. Having reached this agreement during quiet times, it can be called on when things are heating up.

✦

Couple Time!
The Ten Minutes That Can Save Your Marriage

*W*OULD YOU like to turn the worst time of the day into the best time? Would you like to have more romance, warmth, friendship, and relaxation in your life? Then try the following ritual. Taken daily—or as needed—you can make evenings go well, and stay happily married. No kidding!

When you and/or your partner arrive home in the evening, you may have gotten into the habit of putting off relaxation until things are over with—meals, housework, kids, etc. This may work fine when the kids are little and in bed by seven, but not for long; as they get older, you wait longer to be together again.

In the old days, husbands and wives were together more of the time, and got into a rhythm together. The widely differing tempo of our workdays apart means that when we come back together in the family home, we're spinning like tops at different speeds. So it's hard to feel connected. In fact many couples positively clash all night, only starting to synchronize late in the evening, if they have any energy or motivation left!

Therefore, we need to make sure that we DO get synchronized as soon as we can. The way to do this is as follows:

1. MEET! As soon as you are both home, sit down and take a few minutes out together. And while you're doing this . . .
2. EAT! Have some convenient but substantial snack food—salami, nuts, cheese, fruit, fruitcake, something with body in it to fill the hungry gap and give some instant energy. The next step is . . .
3. KIDS TO ONE SIDE! Children, who are often the only ones who do score any time and attention around dinnertime, have to stay out of the way. If they can do this in the room, fine—if not, send them out of the room. Their turn will come. Be tough on this one! It's only ten minutes.

4. DRINK. If you drink alcohol at all, make this the time for it. A single glass of wine, beer, or sherry, together with the snacks, will help you rapidly slip out of the day's tensions and let your body know this is winding-down time.

5. TALK only if you want to. If you do, be sure to talk about good things. Avoid completely the old competition couples play, called "Who Had the Worst Day?" Either talk positively or sit quietly and enjoy just being there.

Soon you'll be settled enough to want to get on with the evening's activities—you can cook a more leisurely meal, since you are no longer desperately hungry, or be with the kids if you are the one who has been absent all day. You'll find that everything flows better because your whole rhythm, even down to your heartbeat, is more synchronized with your partner's.

This daily ritual is so simple, and yet its effect is profound. It saves marriages. It's as simple as that. Give it a try!

✦

seven

Ages and Stages

DO YOU MEAN THIS IS NORMAL?

Kids DO CHANGE as they grow. What's right to say to a three-year-old could be wrong to say to a seven-year-old, and different again from what you would tell, or require of, a teenager. An idea of stages helps you to know what should be going on at a particular age, and how best to react.

The stages explained in this chapter are adapted from a book called *Self Esteem: A Family Affair,* by Jean Illsley-Clarke (see *References,* p. 163, for details). I've discussed them with thousands of parents and the most frequent response has been "Aaaaahhh! That's exactly right!" and, sometimes, "If only we'd known!"

The stages of child development

✎ 0–6 months	Can I trust these people?
✎ 6–18 months	Exploring the world
✎ 18 months–3 years	Learning to think
✎ 3–6 years	Other people
✎ 6–12 years	I did it my way!
✎ 12–18 years	Practicing being an adult

Let's look at them in more detail.

Can I trust these people? (0–6 months)

The human baby arrives like a being from another planet. Its first thoughts and feelings are pretty blurry, but they are very much to do with:

"Am I safe?"

"Who's gonna feed me?"

"What happened to my waterbed?"

"Those people look nice. How can I keep them around?"

"What's that yucky feeling I'm sitting in?"

It is no use making demands of the new baby, or criticizing it, since it is still just "taking it all in." It needs you to guess its needs (to be changed, fed, cuddled, burped, carried around), since it has no way of telling you what it wants.

It's important that you don't ignore its cries for help, since it will learn to become passive and depressed if ignored for long. It's equally important to let it *start* to cry heartily for a moment or two, so that it learns that it can *do something* to get its needs met, that its cries will bring help. A child who is always fed *before* it says it's hungry may have trouble knowing what it wants later in life.

Massaging and cuddling the baby, making noises to it, looking at its face and smiling, all make for a happier, brighter child who subsequently sleeps, feeds, and learns more easily. Massage has been found to cure constipated babies with amazing speed. (Stand well clear!)

Notice how babies from many of the technologically advanced cultures are carried around in slings and carry-bags? One Balinese tradition is the first "setting down to earth" of a new baby—it does not take place until the child is six months old. Before this it is never out of somebody's arms! We would find this rather difficult, but it's worthwhile carrying babies as much of the time as we can.

Exploring the world! (6–18 months)

This is the time when, at no charge to you, the child begins to educate himself. He moves out into the big, beautiful world, tasting, grabbing, pushing, carrying, pulling, and eating everything in sight.

You can save yourself enormous amounts of energy by creating a *safe, child-proof* zone in your house, so that you don't need to be always saying, "*Don't.*" Put the stereo up high somewhere, postpone the new wallpaper and your child will be free to wander in peace (yours).

The Exploring Stage
Goes Wrong

*J*N THE mid-seventies, I was a very inexperienced psychology graduate who knew more about rats than about children.

I began work as a school guidance counselor. My role, according to my superiors, was to take children who, teachers felt, were stupid. I was to administer quaint little tests and then tell the teachers how stupid these children were. This was supposed to be helpful.

I don't really blame my superiors for devising this role. Being responsible for the psychological well-being of three thousand children in nine schools was daunting, and the little tests gave one something concrete to do.

I decided to do something more helpful than just IQ tests. I recruited and trained mothers to coach kids who had fallen behind in reading. I gave talks to teachers about self-esteem. I listened patiently to harassed parents. One day, I went on a home visit to the mother of a boy who was acting up at school. The home was out in the country and looked run-down.

I took off my tie before going in. I talked rather awkwardly with the boy's mom: she looked very old and tired. On the worn, dusty linoleum in the kitchen where we talked, a toddler sat looking dully up at us. There was not a Lego block or any other toy in sight. From time to time the child tugged open a cupboard and pulled at the utensils inside. The mother would stand up, scold the child, slam the cupboard door, and continue talking.

As I drove home, I felt angry and helpless. That mom's idea of a good toddler was a silent, still toddler. I knew that

without toys to play with and without encouragement to
play, or books to look at or stories to hear, that child, too,
would be on the guidance counselor's list before many
years had elapsed: "suspected mentally deficient."

✦

Children at this age need lots to do and to play with—not
expensive toys, just interesting odds and ends. They need to be
free of demands to perform, such as sitting up primly, being
cute, or being toilet trained (the sphincter muscles that control
your child's "outlets" are not yet sufficiently developed for full
control).

Physically, toddlers can be tiring, so this is a good age for you
to start getting breaks of a few hours yourself, to rest and do
your exploring!

Learning to think (18 months–3 years)

Now the child is starting to use reasoning. It's a good time to
give simple explanations for things: "The kitten gets scared
when you squeeze her. I'll show you how to stroke her gently."

Your child is also using anger and learning to say, "No, I
don't want to," "I don't care." This is the age called by some
people "the terrible twos." Parents will need to set clear limits.

The child will test these. The parents must remain firm . . .
and firm . . . and firm.

Work out ahead of time what is really important and what
doesn't matter, to save energy. The child will sometimes want to
be independent and then switch back to being very dependent
again, especially if a new baby arrives on the scene. This is natural, and the child will soon "grow up" again if his needs are met.

Other people (3–6 years)

This is the age when children clearly move from playing alongside other children to playing with other children. It helps if there are other children to learn with. It's also the time of endless questions: when? why? how? what if? why not? and why? again.

When they're chattering your ears off, think of this as language development time, and count the money you're saving in remedial tuition and expensive school fees later in life!

Teasing or ridicule by parents, never a good idea, are particularly unhelpful at this age, when the child is learning how to belong and join in and may easily withdraw.

Fantasy and reality need to be clearly separated: both are okay, but you need to know the difference.

"I'm a monster!"
"You're good at pretending to be a monster!"
Growl! Giggle!

Clear requests for appropriate behavior can be made and are best phrased specifically and positively: "Pick up your cars now" rather than "Don't be untidy."

Vera is the sort of parent who makes you feel like being a little kid. Are you imagining it, or does she actually smell like homemade scones? She's also quick-minded and humorous, and able to put a young psychologist in his place. I decide it's better in this workshop to learn from her than try to teach her, and sure enough I do. Vera recounts how her eight-year-old, Dale, had developed, ever so gradually, a temper that had become a problem to him and to other people. After one particular blow-up of Dale's, Vera had given the matter some careful thought, and then set in motion a profound and original cure.

She took down an old dusty album of family photos (never before seen by the children) and she and Dale looked through them. Vera pointed out the various family patriarchs: Grandfather Les when he was a boy, Great-Uncle Alf, cousin Derek, where they had lived, and what they had done. Dale looked with fascination at the weathered faces and ancient clothing styles, while Vera provided the narrative: "Alf was a good man, but very stubborn; Grandfather had quite a temper when he was a boy, so they say." There was a pause as Dale wondered where this was leading. Vera just turned the pages. "What happened with his temper, Mom?" "Oh, he just grew out of it, I suppose. Look, here's his football team . . ."

Soon the other children came in, and Vera left them with the photos, and went to get the tea. Dale, of course, though he could be stubborn at times, never lost his temper again. He just grew out of it, I suppose.

I did it my way! (6–12 years)

What makes it possible for a six- to twelve-year-old to navigate the world of school, friends, and life, generally, is his or her knowledge of the way things work and the "rules of life." These rules can be anything from "If I share my toys with her she'll be my friend" to "If I don't take my raincoat I'll get wet, and might get a cold and miss out on going ice skating on Saturday."

Parents will help by being firm on those rules that are important, but negotiating and compromising on those that are negotiable. The child thus learns the give-and-take skills that make up so much of adult life.

Challenging and arguing with the child, especially if you are not domineering but genuinely interested, will help the child refine her or his thinking abilities and better understand other people's needs. Self-care by parents is essential so that they can continue this challenging and hassling job while maintaining warmth and good humor.

Practicing being an adult (12–18 years)

Hard as it may seem (or perhaps you're glad?), this is the age of moving away from family, and moving in again, and away again, practicing for the real jump into adult life. Although the child does not yet actually leave, his interests and energies are increasingly falling outside the family.

Parents also need to have their own interests away from parenting, so that they are not tempted to dominate or be over-involved with their child's world, or to use their child in place of adult company. This is particularly important for single parents.

Some parents feel resentful that this is just a taxi-driving stage—which reflects more on our public transportation systems (or lack thereof) and the dangers of our streets at night than anything else. Taxi-ing at least provides a good opportunity to talk.

Three important things are happening:

+ The teenager moves forward like the tide—in waves, in and out. One minute he is independent, another wanting to be fed and nursed. One minute he is impressively reasonable, another rebellious and argumentative. Knowing that this will happen makes it easier to handle. Despite the waves, the tide is making progress.
+ Sexuality is blossoming. A young person needs to hear that sex is good, that sexuality is welcome and healthy, and that it carries some decision-making responsibilities. Parents should not act seductively, or respond to seductiveness from the young person.

✦ The break is going to come. Some young adults move out easily and slowly, but most don't! You can recognize that the young person may need to create and maintain disagreement in order to create the energy to break loose. Don't take this too personally. Like giving birth, releasing young adults is a little painful but well worth the trouble.

And remember, *practicing* being an adult is not the same as *actually* being one. At thirteen or even nineteen, young people can make life-harming mistakes, and get in over their heads with sexuality, drugs or alcohol, peer pressure, and safety, and so still need your close attention. Through discussion and friendly involvement, you oh-so-gradually let them prove their growing ability to handle situations. The biggest single problem of American parents today is the foolish idea that you just have to be a friend to your children. Kids need parents, not another pal. This means being able and willing to say no, to challenge faulty thinking, and to expect accountability. Don't expect the teen years to be less demanding than the toddler years—it's just a different kind of involvement.

The Dopey Time

*A*ROUND THIRTEEN years of age, most teenagers go through a phase of amazing dopeyness. What is happening is that the puberty hormones are just cranking up, and the sudden growth spurt begins to disorganize their nervous system. Look for the signs: A normally very careful boy knocks over the sugar bowl. A girl goes to school with one sock. They are frequently found about the house standing in a daze, not knowing where they were going or why. In short, a competent twelve-year-old suddenly becomes a hopeless and helpless thirteen.

If you don't know about this stage, you might get very irritated, or think that all your efforts have been wasted. But be patient and kind—they really can't help it. The stage usually lasts only a few months, and all you can do is manage them along, draw lists, help them with their homework. Don't nag too much. It's also a nice gentle phase, when you can be close and affectionate. Soon they will be into the fighting fourteens, so enjoy this stage while it lasts!

✦

Kids and TV— the Great Debate

*M*OST KIDS watch a lot of TV. In fact, the average child now spends much more time in front of the TV than she spends at school! Not only is the time spent a concern, but also what is watched. A child, by his mid-teens, will have seen tens of thousands of violent incidents, and thousands of deaths, portrayed in cartoon and realistic form—and this is only in children's viewing hours.

The exposure to violence and cheap life values is the most frequent parental concern about TV watching by kids. The next is what it stops kids from doing—it takes up time that they would normally spend running, jumping, playing, talking, reading, and being creative—if they weren't beguiled by the hypnotic flow of the TV screen.

If you're a parent, I ask you to try just one thing—to watch your kids as they watch TV. You may find it a little chilling to see the slightly open-mouthed, blank-eyed stare that kids develop after a time. They are clearly in an "altered state"; never, in any area of life will you see children so passive and absorbent. By comparison, when reading books, their minds work vigorously as they imagine what the words conjure up. Driving in the car, playing in the yard, going to a circus, they are animated and interactive, "chewing up" the world with their minds. But in front of the TV they soon drift into that old stare again, the active part of their brain "out to lunch." Take a look for yourself and judge whether you like what you see.

Young children are particularly affected by what they see on the screen. We once had a four-year-old staying at our house, and he came in for a cuddle before bedtime. We were watching a comedy show, and an add came on in which an ET-type creature's hand came out of a cupboard, rejected some chips and some lollipops, but grabbed the child and pulled it in—then burped! It was subtly done, with no real violence—just wry adult humor. I glanced at the child's face, though, just to check, and noticed his jaw very set.

"Are you okay, Ben?"

"Go away!"

"What are you angry about?"

"That boy got eaten!"

Then he started to cry, and we spent a good five minutes comforting him and trying to make light of the incident. We were touched by Ben's compassion and a little ashamed that we'd exposed him to unnecessary pain. We worried that he would have nightmares or trouble sleeping. Older kids, though, will watch horrific scenes without apparent reaction. Are they desensitized? Is that a bad thing? Of course it is.

Guidelines

If you are a little alarmed and want to do something about what your children watch, here are some suggestions for assessing kids' TV:

Language—Not just swearing, but the quality and richness of verbal skills. Here's a simple test: listen to your child's program for a minute or two without the picture (or go around the corner and listen to the dialogue). Is that the kind of talking you want your child to learn? "Aaargh! Urghh! Take that! I'll teach you to . . ."

Imagination—Some kids only know how to play very restricted games—shooting, screaming, hitting. Perhaps this is a symptom that this is all they are watching on TV. It's possible to select kids' TV shows with a much wider range of themes. PBS shows, nature shows—they pass the best test of kids' fare: you can stand to watch them yourself! Some movies and programs for kids are simply stunning in imagination, depth, and challenge.

Values—This means the hidden message in the program, which has a powerful effect on kids because it is largely unconscious. Common value problems include:

✦ Bad guys and good guys. Some people are villains: they have deep voices and look funny; they are all bad; it's okay to kill them. Some people are all good: they are handsome and bland.

✦ Conflict is always a result of the bad guys being mean, until the good guys get revenge. It's okay to hurt the bad guys for what they've done. Revenge is sweet. There is no negotiation or middle ground. There are no reasons or sides to the conflict. Action—the more violent the better—is the answer to conflict.

✦ Sex roles—This is the one that really should have gone away by now. But still, in shows from *Superman* to *The Saint,* the girls are cute, beautiful, have high-pitched voices, and need rescuing. Boys or men have weapons and are action-oriented, always flying the spaceship, making the decisions, rescuing the girls. And they don't cry—ever!

Advertising—Are the shows produced by toy companies to be, in effect, half-hour ads for toy figures or accessories? Are the ads all for junk food or overpriced fad toys?

News—Don't mistake the news for education. It is actually a form of entertainment, and often gives a distorted and unrealistic view of the world. It's not suitable for primary-age children, and we don't think, in its present form, it does much for adults either. Watching the news can make you paranoid and depressed—and ill-informed about the world we live in.

What about educational TV?

Research has found that *Sesame Street* and similar programs work much better if parents watch alongside their children, from time to time, singing the songs or commenting on the characters, and helping their kids "participate" with the program—in this way helping them to avoid the glazed-eye syndrome. The makers of these programs deliberately lace them with subtler humor and ironies to interest adult viewers. They also have rock stars and other celebrities as guests to ensure that parents will turn the shows on and occasionally watch them with their kids.

In summary

Has it occured to you that the purpose of television is to make children unhappy with who they are and what they have? That it's a direct attack on their self-esteem and happiness—for commercial gain.

Many parents now restrict what their kids watch in quantity and quality. Parents of children under three often have no TV at all, or just a few favorite shows. For older children, they allocate an hour per day and help them choose which programs they will watch. This encourages children to plan, be selective, and savor "their" program rather than just watching an endless stream.

A TV that just plays all the time in the living room guarantees that no good conversations will ever occur, since no one will ever give each other their full attention. Switch it off. A TV in a child's bedroom means they will go to sleep every night full of disturbing, jumbled, and mind-numbing images and ideas. Its the death of imagination and peace of mind. Keep TV out of bedrooms and playrooms until they are well into their teens.

✦

How to Stop Whining Kids

*H*AVE YOU noticed how some adults have really pleasant voices? And that some children also have melodious, clear tones that are a pleasure to listen to? And have you also noticed that there is nothing harder on your ears than a kid who is always whining. Talking through their nose? "Aaaaawwwwwww, Mohhhhhhhhmmmmmmm?"

Did you know that the tone of voice we use—as adults or kids—is simply a habit? Not just a habit of voice, but also of attitude to life! Whining comes from the "helpless" part of us that wants others to fix everything, that is never satisfied, that loves to complain. Whenever we talk with a whine, we will feel this way too. Whining kids, if uninterrupted, will grow into whining adults. (Behind every nagging husband or moaning wife is a parent who gave in to a whiner.) But whining can be stopped overnight! Here's how:

First you have to understand how the pattern starts. It's simple enough. A child asks us for something, first all quietly, then loudly. We say no, or else ignore them. They then move into phase two—they rev up into full-scale whining. It's probably accidental at first—they discover by chance a tone of voice that we just can't ignore! We will often give in to them, if only for some peace and quiet. Before you know it, you have a whining kid.

So what do you do?

1. TELL 'EM. Next time they start whining at you, make direct eye contact. Then ask them straight out: "use a normal voice, please."

2. TEACH 'EM HOW. Find out if they actually know how to speak in a lower-sounding voice—firm, but deeper in note. Try them out until they get it right. Demonstrate for them so they can hear what you mean.

3. MAKE IT STICK. Start the campaign. Whenever they whine at you for anything, say to them, "Use a normal voice." You are getting them to realize that whining is not normal, for them, or anyone else. Make sure that they get what they are asking for only by asking more positively.

Of course, don't give in to them if it doesn't suit you—they still have to learn to take no for an answer. "I liked the way you spoke when you asked me for a cookie, but I'm sorry, you'll have to wait for dinner."

✦

∴ **eight** ∾

Energy and How to Save It

GOOD NEWS—

YOUR CHILDREN NEED YOU HEALTHY AND HAPPY.

♦

$\mathcal{J}$ ONCE LIVED for a time in a coastal village of Papua New Guinea. Children there did not live with their own parents but moved about from house to house as they wished! Ten-year-olds could be seen carrying babies or tending cooking fires. By fourteen they were doing adult work with confidence and pride. As the newest and most interesting thing in the village, I had a dozen or so kids sleeping on my veranda. When tropical diarrhea struck in the small hours of the night, I had to pick my way out through a carpet of small brown bodies.

It occurred to me that this would be an easy place to be a parent, since the work and pleasure of parenting was shared by the whole village. In fact, any adult who was present *was* a parent.

In our society, parenting is not shared, and it's not safe for small children to move about the community.

It's easy to feel, then, that you have to become "Superparent" and somehow meet, by yourself, all the needs of your kids for entertainment, education, love and affection, food, drink, safety, clothing, and cleaning. If you're the one who stays at home with the kids, you feel overdomesticated and housebound and yearn for adult company. If you're the one who goes out and makes the money, you feel like a workhorse, with too little home and family in your life. It's little wonder that many of us, especially when we have two or more children under age five, are almost permanently exhausted, irritable, and in borderline health.

When we feel well, and in good company, and healthy and rested, we can give to our children and enjoy doing it. But when we feel tired, sick, lonely, and overburdened, there is a point at which kids become a threat, competitors in the struggle for survival. This condition can easily be dangerous, to you, your marriage, and the safety of your kids.

Overstretched parents can sometimes reach a point at which they can parent no longer. It is vital that you learn to take care of yourself: only then can you parent well. Your kids need you happy and healthy. This brief chapter will tell you how to be and stay that way.

WE ALL NEED "FUEL"

I OFTEN TALK with parents who don't understand why they aren't coping. They expect superhuman performance without realizing that we human beings need "fuel." We don't just run on food: we need "energy" in the form of love, recognition, touch, and talking with others.

Every person you talk to or meet either takes energy away from you or gives you energy. That's why we speak of some people as being "draining." It's also the reason we dread certain people calling us, or drive for an hour just to see a special friend who makes us feel good.

Kids can give energy back to us, but for the most part it is right and proper that *we recharge them*. However, when we are their only source of refueling and we dry up on them, something is bound to happen.

Think for a moment. Where is your energy tank right now, as you are reading this book?

Is this where you usually keep it? Are you always "running on empty?"

We often treat our bodies as we treat our cars: ten dollars' worth at a time, bald tires, and long overdue for a tune-up!

You might like to look at the people in your life and consider how they help or hinder your fuel reserves. Sometimes people realize that their "friends" are simply "stealing" energy and giving nothing back. Time to find some new friends! People who were once good for us (including parents!) may now be a source of only negative feelings. You can, if you wish, change the way you interact with people so that you move to positive exchanges instead of negative ones.

"Hello, dear, I've had a terrible week!"

"I've had a good one. Let me tell you about it."

"God, there were so many problems at the office today."

"Well, I could listen while you tell me about them. Or would you prefer to plan our next vacation?"

It's a neat strategy and, carried out with good humor, benefits both parties.

With a group of twenty young parents, I once spent a couple of hours listing the ways that parents can "refuel their tanks." We came up with quite a few good ideas.

+ Exchange baby-sitting time with another couple you know and trust.
+ Learn to be boring to your children so they leave you in peace for a while.

✦ Spend ten minutes with your partner when he or she comes home from work: exchange *good news* or just be together. (If the kids can sit quietly, they can be there; if not, send them into another room.)

✦ Spend half an hour of *full-attention* time with children each day, instead of hours of begrudged half-attention. Let children plan and look forward to what they want to do with you in *their* half-hour.

✦ Learn to *switch off* in a comfortable way, so that you relax and think nice thoughts as you do housework, commute to work, or whatever.

✦ Cook food the way *you* like it sometimes, instead of always eating kids' food.

✦ Play *your* music.

✦ Spend plenty of time with other parents.

✦ Be clear about what you are asking of your partner: affection, sex, or just company. Try to meet and understand each other's needs as they arise. If you usually just talk when you're tense, try massage. If you usually just touch, try talking.

✦ On a regular basis, do one activity that is not concerned with being a parent but is an *adult-satisfying activity,* just for you.

✦ Have a good escapist book to unwind with at bedtime or a mid-afternoon nap.

✦ Use all the kinds of support and help around: neighborhood houses, child health centers, fitness clubs (especially the friendly, noncommercial kind), sports, playgroups, daycare centers, parenting classes.

✦ Use a daycare center for "*self-time,*" instead of only for rushing around the shops or to a job.

✦ Learn that "messy is beautiful" and give up "tidy house" ideals for a few years. (You can always leave a vacuum cleaner by the door and say to visitors, "Gee, I was just about to start cleaning up!")

+ Have kids' areas of the house, where valuable things are not around and surfaces and furniture are easy to clean. This saves the wasted energy of a thousand "don'ts" a day.
+ Have tidy and beautiful areas of the house (even if it's only your bedroom) where kids aren't allowed to go—so that you have somewhere nice to be.
+ Talk, solve problems, figure out plans with your partner in the living room, sitting down, face to face, with the kids out of the way. Don't make bed the worrying place. Bed is for better purposes than that.

Mothering Mothers

*W*HEN SOME newborn babies "meet" their mothers, they do not bond well, and changing and feeding are a struggle in which baby and mother are tense and unhappy. Some Austrailian hospitals have introduced a program for rebonding that is beautiful in its simplicity, and symbolic of the whole parenting process. The staff realized that mother and baby were caught in a vicious circle. They solved this by sitting the mother on a bean bag and the father behind her on a chair. The father gently massaged the mother's shoulders and back, enabling her to relax. The mother held and stroked the infant, perhaps feeding it, too. If the mother was a single parent, then a male member of staff would massage the mother instead; and if the father felt tense or awkward, then a physiotherapist might even stand behind him and massage his shoulders.

The unique nature of touch, giving both energy and reassurance, enables humans to soften and move out of tense patterns. It is so often forgotten . . . but it beats tranquillizers every time!

✦

BUT I DON'T HAVE TIME FOR ME!

THE PARENTS WHO get most stressed are those who set very high standards and put their own needs far down the list: "But doctor, I don't understand it. I had just finished redecorating the spare room and baking the three-tiered cake for Tyson's party when this awful headache started. Could you give me something for it because I have to hurry back and get ready for the in-laws' coming to stay for a month!"

In fact, there are three simple responsibilities you have as a parent. You have to:

+ take care of yourself
+ take care of your partnership
+ take care of your kids

People used to think that, to be a parent, you had to make huge sacrifices and become a doormat. Then we swung the other way and people assumed kids were a kind of fashion accessory that could be fit in after work, cocktails, and going to the gym! Let's be clear about this—You should only have children if you are willing to come second in your own list of priorities for about twenty years. At the same time, you have to keep a little for yourself and for your partnership because this is the engine that drives the whole thing along. There is a very old word that you don't hear much anymore–sacrifice–which is what successful parents and partners do routinely, not out of martyrhood, but to achieve a much bigger satisfaction in the long run. This concept has gotten somewhat lost in the me-generation era of looking after number one. Lifelong love, smiling grandchildren, and kids who want to be around you all come from giving up many short term rewards. It's your choice.

Looking after your partnership reminds you that you're a valued and attractive adult, not just a child-minder or a breadwinner in the other person's eyes. You have a sense of stability that enables you to relax, but you have enough growth and change taking place to enable you to remain interested in and excited by your partner.

Looking after your kids flows naturally from the above: if you feel that you have chosen parenting as one of your goals, if you are self-caring and have partnerships and friendships that sustain you and remind you of your worth, then giving to children will come easily. Your tank will often be full and your children won't need to start panic buying! End of sermon.

Saving Energy with the "Soft No"

*J*EREMY IS two-and-a-half, and a handful. He seems to have learned infant-assertiveness, and makes demands over and over until something happens— whether it's to have ice cream for breakfast, to interrupt Mom on the phone, or to get that shiny toy at the supermarket checkout.

Luckily, his mother, Allie, is discovering how to deal with all of this. Firstly, she knows that this is a normal developmental stage for children of Jeremy's age, and that it won't last forever. Secondly, she has just mastered the "soft-no" technique, and has become invincible!

She sees other mothers struggle with their two-year-olds, and sees them caught up in rising tension:

I wannit! No
I WANNIT! NO!
I WANNIT I WANNIT I WANNIT!
NO YOU CAN'T HAVE IT!

The mothers become angry and tense and upset with themselves, assuming that they must match their infants' red-faced loudness in order to win.

Allie, however, does it differently. She simply says no, quite softly (knowing that children have excellent hearing). If Jeremy persists, she says it again, equally softly, at the same time relaxing her shoulders and softening her whole body (a trick which took a few hours to master). If Jeremy shouts, especially in a public place, she imagines herself carrying him bodily to the car, but at the same time softens and smiles inwardly. She controls her own feelings, rather than letting little Jeremy control them. The temptation to yell at him occasionally returns, but imagining the way he would enjoy this victory soon removes the temptation.

Allie is puzzled that just as she has mastered the "soft-no" skill, Jeremy seems to have stopped his hassling.

✦

Food and Kids' Behavior

*W*OULD YOU change your kids' diet, if you knew it would make them do really well at school, be calm and happy in themselves, and twice as pleasant to be around? Of course you would. Did you know that poor food intake is thought to be a major factor in juvenile crime? And did you know that the same changes to diet can help you to feel better, have more energy, and perhaps avoid being overweight without eating any less?

Sometimes it's important to go back to the basics—and there's nothing more basic than food. What we feed to our children, and when, has a profound effect.

Here are some simple guidelines on the psychological effects of food:

1. CHOOSE FOOD THAT GIVES STEADY ENERGY. Food serves two purposes. It provides nutrients for growing and for repairing our bodies, and it also gives us energy for physical and mental activity. Most people these days provide their kids with a range of foods to give a nourishing diet. But it's also important to give the right kind of energizing food—complex carbohydrates, and protein foods, which give a steady, daylong energy release. This kind of diet will prevent fatigue, promote a steady, focused state of mind, and help children to feel settled and easy. In particular, children need to eat complex carbohydrates (whole grain foods), high protein foods, and perhaps some fresh foods such as fruit, for breakfast each day.

2. EAT IT BEFORE YOU NEED IT. That's right—break-fast! Breakfast is the meal that will provide energy throughout the day. Eating substantial foods in the afternoon or evening may nourish you and your kids, but the energy input will be wasted. Eating your main food intake just before you become active will also avoid obesity—food goes straight into the bloodstream, where it's needed. When children or adults eat a big meal in the evening, then just sit around or sleep; the food is laid down into their fatty reserves. People can eat just as much, but by changing WHEN they eat it, they'll find that this will reduce weight problems.

   We suggest that you experiment. Give your children protein foods such as eggs, meat, or fish with their breakfast each day for two weeks. (If they complain they aren't hungry at breakfast time, give them less for dinner the night before!) See for yourself how much more settled and happy they are at home and school.

3. AVOID "QUICK BURNOUT" FOODS. Sugar and refined sugary foods have a remarkably unpleasant effect on kids' behavior. Many children have simply too much energy minutes after eating such rapid-release foods. They become edgy, hyperactive, and just plain naughty. Blood tests show that this energy release peaks early, and the child's blood sugar drops below where it started, as the body struggles to cope. Thus children have a mid-morning sag, in which they cannot concentrate, and become lazy and unfocused.

4. AVOID CHEMICALS, DYES, AND PRESERVATIVES. Additives and dyes in foods have complex and individual effects.

In addition to observing what your child reacts to, you'll want to keep in mind that some foods are generally a problem for almost every child. The need to reduce sugar has already been mentioned especially at breakfast and lunchtime. Tartrazine (E102), which is found in yellow-dyed foods, can cause violent hours of hyperactivity in children. Phosphates (found in processed foods such as hot dogs, commercial hamburgers, processed cheese, instant soup, and toppings) are also strongly implicated.

The simplest and most effective thing you can do is feed your kids good food earlier in the day, so they just won't get as hungry for junk. Likewise, if your child is going to a party where the parents are still living in the 1950s diet-wise (soft drinks, cakes, ice-cream, and lollipops!), then feed your kids before they go–and minimize the damage!

In the September 1998 edition of *New Internationalist*, a study on 3,000 young offenders found that they had a 70–80% reduction in criminal behavior over twelve months, while on high nutrition/low junk food diet. We will need less police, psychiatrists, and jails when people start having a good breakfast.

Appendix

How you can help if you're a teacher, a politician,
a grandparent, neighbor, or friend.

✦

If YOU'RE AN elementary school teacher: How to counteract negative programming in the children you teach

By the time a child gets to kindergarten you will be able to recognize "negative programming" very clearly. Here are the main indicators:

+ a child who hangs back from other children, looks sad or agitated, and does not respond to overtures of friendship from other children
+ a child who joins in but, when presented with a learning task or activity, will not try it and looks fearful or distracted if approached on a one-to-one basis
+ a child who lashes out at other children and reacts inappropriately when spoken to (for example, by laughing when chastised) and does not seem to have positive exchanges with other children

You may have children in your class who fall into one of these three categories, or you may find children with a combination of the three.

For the sake of simplicity, let's look at them one at a time.

THE SAD AND LONELY CHILD

IT IS MOST useful to regard this kind of child as having missed out on affection and on being valued and affirmed in the early part of life (0–2 years). He needs positive messages that are not tied to performance but are simply strokes for "being," such as "Hello, Eric, nice to see you." A friendly touch or hug with the child, being careful not to make him seem different from the others, also provides reassurance.

Such strategies, spread out over some days and weeks, should result in the child visibly relaxing and loosening up in the classroom and then beginning to initiate contact with you–showing you work, smiling at you as you scan the room, speaking to you, and so on.

THE SELF-CRITICAL CHILD WHO WON'T GIVE THINGS A TRY

THIS CHILD MAY have had her needs met in the early part of life but has been subjected to verbal put-downs consistently since she was old enough to listen (which was, of course, very young). The pattern often tends to occur when a mother has a second baby and shifts to being verbally critical of the first child.

Many parents, especially when they themselves are having a tough time, will put their children down as a matter of course, almost every time they speak to them. The children who have grown up in such situations (probably at least one in ten children) will actually say things like "I'm stupid," "I can't," or "I'm a dumb-dumb" if asked why they won't attempt some new task.

The remedy will be obvious to you: give positive affirmations very consistently to these children. Ideally, give positive messages both for performance and for just being. For example, "You did that really well," "I like your ideas for paintings," as well as "It's nice to see you this morning!" or just plain "Hello." Don't gush, though—make quiet, understated comments that they can tolerate.

You will have to make sure that you avoid using put-downs with the child (who may actually invite them) and that you use assertive statements rather than "you" statements to control the child.

For example, use "Go and get your bag now!" instead of "You're so forgetful, Anna."

For a really lasting impact, though, the child's parents will need some help, too. You will probably find, if they come to the school, that they are tired, overworked, and possibly resentful and defensive. Your best approach would be a casual and friendly chat before broaching the problem, rather than a "Your kid is a problem" full-frontal attack!

You can simply explain that you have noticed that their child's self-esteem is low and that he or she may be sensitive to put-downs and in need of more praise.

Parents of kids in this category will be the ones most helped by reading this book. You could lend them a copy!

THE CHILD WHO IS AGGRESSIVE TOWARD OTHER KIDS AND SARCASTIC TO YOU

I SAVED THIS one till last! This child can be best understood as having been fully hooked on a "negative" culture, being both handled in an aggressive way and shown by example only negative ways of relating. It is very likely that the child's parents fight routinely, in words if not in actions.

Significantly, the child is not *choosing* to interact using aggression; it may be the only way he or she knows *how* to interact.

It is very important to realize that, initially, this kind of child will *not* often respond to warmth and praise (but it's worth a try).

The teacher must first of all establish a bond through the mode the child can hear—that of firm engagement. This must be done, of course, without using put-downs.

Thus, in the early weeks, a firm but friendly approach and a clear request for behavior ("Hey, John, come over here to get a book," "Sit down now and start your drawing") are the necessary reactions from you.

The way to establish a beneficial and significant relationship with an aggressive child is to persist—firmly and without becoming angry or irritated. Eye contact, especially with humor behind the eyes as you reinforce your firmness, will signal that you are powerful enough to contain the child, so that he or she can begin to relax.

Once this relationship has been established, then positive messages can be added for doing positive things. This differs from what the parents may have done: only noticing the child when he or she acted up.

These children are often the most responsive to having special roles (such as "equipment collector")—roles with a genuine responsibility and privilege. As they develop a "friendship" with you, that is, the skill of exchanging positive messages, they will be able to extend this to other children.

IF YOU'RE A HIGH SCHOOL TEACHER

NEGATIVELY PROGRAMMED CHILDREN are very much in evidence in high schools. In fact, the nature of secondary school can easily worsen the programming.

Often, high schools are so factory-like that young people feel they are a nobody, doing what they're told and producing things.

High schools often have huge numbers (often over a thousand in a school, although research suggests that three to four hundred is the ideal size); no home base (students are never on their own territory and often even change groupings so that they do not stay with the same friends); and impersonal teaching (learning from so many different teachers, who teach so many classes that they would be hard-pressed even to know your name, let alone to care about you).

In my research I have found that students have four major problems with high school: the work; sarcasm and put-downs from teachers; loneliness; and put-downs and aggression from other kids. It is appropriate for us to address here the last three of these problems.

SARCASM AND PUT-DOWNS FROM TEACHING STAFF

THIS IS A symptom of unhappiness and frustration in the teacher. Few non-teachers have any idea of the stress and difficulty of teaching in high schools in the nineties. Teachers come a close second to psychiatrists in the rate of work-caused physical and mental breakdowns.

A large, faceless school isn't any happier for the teacher than for the kids. High schools, fueled by the breakdown of families and the rise of epidemic unemployment and its hardships, are often physically menacing, emotionally harrowing places, unless very concerted and innovative efforts are being made to humanize the school environment.

Sarcasm and aggressive attacks on children are used for two reasons. One is that they simply relieve the teacher's inner pressures: if the teacher was a happier person they would not take place. The second is that control of kids is a constant preoccupation and sarcasm works in getting kids to behave, at least in the short term.

One last plea. We all lose our temper and sound off from time to time. Kids can handle this. It's constant criticizing that hurts. If you don't basically like and enjoy kids, please don't be a teacher.

Isolation is also epidemic in high schools. Observe the school grounds or corridors closely during a break and you will notice that some students will be visibly alone, others will be attached to cliques and groupings of students, but only loosely so, tagging along but rarely interacting with the others.

Boys will be more tolerant of appendages to their groups: girls tend to include or exclude more decisively. For this reason, you will also see pairs or trios of girls who stay together simply out of mutual loneliness, sometimes barely even talking.

LONELINESS

IN THE CLASSROOM you will notice that some children lack even the most basic conversational skills. They will only be able to manage a mumbled word or two if spoken to and would never initiate a conversation unaided. Only recently are some English, speech, and drama teachers beginning to tackle these vital skills.

Lonely kids tend to go unnoticed; their more noisy and aggressive counterparts are actually better off, since they at least get some of the attention they are seeking. It may take a second look at the classes you teach to spot the loners and wordless ones; they will certainly be there.

If you are willing to "prioritize" the one or two lonely children in each class, deliberately making contact with them and showing an interest in their work, without drawing down on them the spotlight of class attention, then even this small amount of attention will go a long way to help them gain confidence.

Any efforts to humanize the school experience—such as homerooms and home groups, excursions, camps, peer support networks, and teaching in the areas of social skills, relationships, and self-esteem—will be of immense benefit. High school is for many children the last chance to climb out of a negative program for life. Do what you can!

PEER AGGRESSION, IN ACTION AND WORDS

BULLYING IS NOT caused by "bad kids." The problem is, in fact, always a symptom of the adult system in which the children live. An oppressive situation, at home or school, leads to the "victims" taking it out on each other.

People pass on their bad feelings—usually to someone further down the pecking order. If this dynamic is not understood, school authorities try to stop the persecution with more persecution and the result is even greater tension and violence in the system.

Where teachers are given proper facilities and support in their jobs, and children are treated with firmness but allowed to keep their self-respect, then bullying of kids by kids rapidly dies away. Although material conditions in a school are important, they in no way compare with *how people treat each other,* from the top down.

School is not usually the source of children's more serious problems. Nonetheless, it does have a way of compounding the misery! Unhappy kids don't learn. Studies which I have helped to carry out in Australia found that illiterate adults had almost universally suffered problems of adjustment *before they even entered school.* The school, however, failed to remedy the fearfulness and low self-esteem of these children, which in turn became a handicap in their learning to read and write. (Over forty million Americans have significant literacy problems.)

The failure of schools to help problem children is rarely the fault of the classroom teacher. The fault lies in the whole method of "factory schooling": we attempt to teach children in herds of thirty to forty at a time, and wonder that so many do not learn well. We are the only culture in history that has taken such an approach to educating our young; thousands of years ago Native Americans were teaching young people on a one-to-one basis and had few failures or dropouts.

IN SUMMARY

NO TEACHER, HOWEVER dedicated, can be both the emotional support and learning stimulus that thirty children need in order to learn well. Soon the day will come when we reassess education and learn to flood our schools with skilled adults, volunteer and paid, trained and training, so that each child gets his or her due. Until then, education will be an uphill battle, with many casualties.

Since you are a caring teacher (or you would not be reading this) and since you want to do as much as you can now, let me conclude by urging you to:

+ eliminate put-downs from your classroom and use assertive methods of control

✦ when faced with problem children, who may already be taking much of your time and nervous energy, consider using the methods outlined in this chapter

✦ be sure to meet your *own* needs for positive strokes and affirmation. You are an endangered species and American children need you healthy and alive!

If You're a Politician or Community Activist!

A family is not an island. Healthy families can only exist in a society that supports their needs. Society can be seen as a kind of gigantic social club, to which we all pay membership fees and where we attend a lot of meetings, and in return receive various benefits.

The social club is far from perfect. Not only is it disorganized, but members with vested interests different from our own work constantly change its direction in their favor. We thus have to work hard to make sure that we and others get our part of the bargain, while at the same time being cooperative enough so that the club does not collapse.

Parents in particular find that they need to keep dealing with the world to get a fair deal for their children. Thus, as well as directing energies "inward" to improve family life by playing with and educating children, parents may find themselves focusing "outward" to society, being on school committees, neighborhood organizations, right through to committing strongly to political, environmental, or other causes.

Naturally, people can overbalance in either direction. On one extreme we find the uninvolved family that does not venture into community life, and can thus be herded like sheep into an increasingly totalitarian state. In contrast, we find parents who are so politically involved (or career-involved, or cause-involved) that they have no family life and so become neurotic and burned out, while neglecting their own marriage and kids.

This book has been an "inward" book, dealing with life within the family unit—a worthwhile focus but one needing balance. This brief section looks at how our new understanding of family life affects the wider picture.

In exchange for our membership in society we receive what is sometimes called the "social contract." The family gives its labor, taxes, and in many other ways contributes to society. In fact, the family multiplied by millions IS society. The family, however, often finds that it is in some way being shortchanged—perhaps health care is poor quality or too expensive, there are no social facilities, or jobs do not exist for the family's teenagers. This requires the family to fight for what it needs.

In dozens of parent workshops I have talked about "parents' rights," and found that parents are dissatisfied with services, such as schools, doctors, local government, and so on. Allowing for the natural tendency of humans to enjoy a good grumble, it's clear that many people feel powerless and shortchanged by the society around them, and especially by "the authorities." The concepts of assertiveness apply here too, and we now teach parents through role-play and strategy-rehearsal to deal with vague doctors, rude public servants, arrogant teachers, and so on, and to get their rights in consumer dealings too.

Assertiveness in the wider arena must include organized action, since single voices only have limited power. More and more, in the twenty-first century, people are joining interest groups and movements. No longer do they opt for trivial, time-filling groups (the tennis-court-improvement-cake-bake-auxiliary) nor do they favor larger faceless groups such as traditional political parties, but rather more mid-range movements such as environmental action groups, school involvement groups, and so on.

Politicians should welcome this tendency, since it is the road to real participatory democracy, as well as being a low-cost solution to community development. A caring, close neighborhood does far more to prevent child abuse (through its removal of loneliness and boredom) than any number of doctors and social workers. Self-help groups such as GROW (for mental health), Parents Anonymous (for child protection), Alcoholics Anonymous, Childbirth Education Association, Parents Without Partners, and Vietnam Veterans of America are proliferating, and doing a remarkable job.

There is no doubt that families need material security first. Below a certain income level, no one can raise happy children. However, above a basic level the need changes. What people benefit from most once they are housed and fed adequately is a chance to be connected with others and involved in purposeful activity that has been freely chosen. One often hears the complaint that parents "don't want to get involved." Usually this complaint comes from someone who conducts boring and alienating parent-teacher nights or preachy lectures on how to bring up children! Contrast this with the immense success of parties for looking at and buying plastic bowls and lacy underwear! Clearly people love to involve themselves in friendly, participatory gatherings, and will risk an excess of lunch boxes to do so! It's sad that such trivial gatherings are often the only way to meet the strong needs for belonging and interaction in our vast suburban homelands.

A large-scale statistical study in the United States sought to find out why, in spite of low income, broken homes, and poor housing, some teenagers remained law-abiding and productive, while others became criminal offenders. The only factor that emerged clearly was that those who coped had access to at least one trustworthy and involved adult figure, outside their immediate family. Most often this was through belonging to a club or group led by interested adults. Since incarceration of young offenders costs about $42,000 per person per year, youth work also seems a sound investment.

Let's sum up. If you are a parent, you will often need to get involved with groups and situations outside your own four walls in order to advance your family's interests and secure some kind of future for your children to live in. If you are involved in the community, whether as secretary of a parents-and-friends club, or a politician, then the one thing you must understand is that families need to BELONG. Whatever helps to bond families together and build strong local communities will save money and trouble a hundredfold, and lead to a happier, more self-reliant society in the future. When public money is being spent, prevention is definitely better than cure.

IF YOU'RE A GRANDPARENT, NEIGHBOR, OR FRIEND

PARENTING CAN BE a lonely business. Often it is only those people who live nearby or are close family who see the pressure building up and the negative put-down patterns beginning to develop between parent and child. It's difficult in this position, though, to know how to offer help in a way that won't offend. Let me make some suggestions.

PRACTICAL HELP

THE MOST OBVIOUS way you can help is baby-sitting. Many young parents are exhausted from the sheer endlessness of parenting and earning a living. A couple of hours' relief may be life-saving, and yet is something that parents hesitate to ask for, for fear of imposing on you. Here's a hint: offer to baby-sit "sometimes" and do so, but occasionally say, "No, I won't be able to this week." This lets the parents know that you can say no—and also means you won't be taken for granted! A friend of mine, who is crafty to match her years, offers to baby-sit for some young parents next door only if they agree to use the time for relaxation. Manipulative but effective.

Material help comes next. Our society seems to be built on a pattern whereby we are poor when we are raising our children, and have an excess of money when our children are grown up. In earlier times people were individually poorer, but could *share* in the family's collective property. The loan of all the equipment needed for raising children (strollers, etc.) or other forms of material support is much appreciated by today's young family.

FRIENDSHIP

THERE IS NOTHING like warm, good-humored availability, and a willingness to listen, in a neighbor or friend. Parents accumulate tension and worries as they go along and, with a sympathetic listener, these will tend to pour off like water off a duck's back. If you have the time to listen and inquire, and if you don't rush in with remedies or comparisons, you will visibly notice the relaxation spread on the person's face as he or she talks.

Don't preach, teach, judge, compare, criticize, evaluate. If you feel the urge coming over you, then close your mouth and smile a lot until the feeling passes. Advice can be a blow to the self-esteem of the person receiving it, especially if it wasn't sought in the first place. Even if it's "good" advice, it will have the unpleasant side effect of making the person feel small. Take my advice!

WHAT NOT TO DO

IF YOU ARE the parent's parent, you will be tempted again and again to slip in some of the parenting you overlooked when they were twelve years old, just at the moment when they are floundering and hoping you hadn't noticed. If you do this often your offspring will have to pretend to be coping whenever you're around.

SUPPLEMENTARY PARENTS

MARGARET MEAD ONCE said that little kids and grandparents get on so well because they have a common enemy! Kids do need other adults to give approval and affection at those times when parents are just too overtaxed to respond well. I know of many people who only made it through their childhood because in an otherwise unbearable home life there was one older person nearby who provided a safe harbor. Even the crabbiest grandparent has his value, if only to show that Mom and Dad really are nice people by contrast!

When families are woven in with friends and neighbors, and when people of all generations have access to each other, then we won't need psychologists or departments of social welfare. We'll take care of ourselves.

A Story to End With

A GOOD FRIEND of mine, a paramedic, told me this story about an incident at his house, which is a good one to end this book with. It's about being human and making mistakes and how, as long as we don't quit, things have a way of working out.

Dave had survived a very tough day at work. He was tired, it was hot, the house was a mess. It was getting late in the evening.

His oldest boy, a largish fourteen-year-old, was crowding around in the kitchen in that way that teenage boys seem to, kind of taking up all the space at once. An argument flared up. The father suddenly found himself yelling, "Look, just get out of here. Go to your room. I'm sick of you!"

The boy stormed off to his room. Within seconds, Dave felt utterly ashamed. He had seen the boy's face as he yelled at him, seen his eyelids flinch at the violence of his father's anger. He realized the boy would have been physically afraid at that moment.

He tried to figure out why he had been so angry. It didn't fit the situation. Perhaps it was just the day. Either way, the feeling of shame didn't go away.

After a few minutes, he went up to the boy's bedroom, and said he was sorry. "I shouldn't have yelled at you. You were hassling me, but it didn't deserve me shouting or sending you away. I'm sorry and I'd like to ask your forgiveness."

Ouch! It takes guts to do this; it hurts even just to write it. The boy was very noncomittal. His feelings were hurt, and a few words saying "sorry" were hard to trust. The father left it at that and went downstairs and cleaned up the kitchen.

After twenty minutes or so, he went up to go to bed. He was in the bathroom brushing his teeth when the son ambled past on his way to the toilet. The youngster had a twinkle in his eye, and spoke softly, but very clearly, as he walked through, "How come it's so hard to hate you?"

You invest a lot in your kids, from the sleepless nights early on and the frightening trips to the emergency room, to homework assignments and a million miles of taxi-driving. The great thing is that everything you put in counts, and with a bit of luck, one day they will realize it. Love adds up to something. It's indestructable and immortal and carries on long after your own life is over. Who could ask for more.

References

✦

These are some of the books used as sources or cited in the book:

Axline, Virginia, *Dibs*, Penguin, London, 1980.

Biddulph, Steve and Shaaron, *The Making of Love*, Doubleday, Sydney, 1988.

Embling, John, *Toma Child's Life Regained*, Pelican, New York, 1980.

Gordon, Thomas, *Parent Effectiveness Training*, Plume, New York, 1970.

Illsey-Clarke, Jean, *Self-Esteem: A Family Affair*, Winston, Oak Grove, Minnesota, 1978.

James and Jongeward, *Born to Win*, Addison Wesley Longman, Reading, Massachusetts, 1971.

Liedloff, Jean, *The Continuum Concept*, Futura, London, 1975.

Pipher, Mary, *The Shelter of Each Other*, Ballantine, New York, 1997.

Schiff, Jacqui, *All Our Children*, Ballantine, New York, 1983.

York, David and Phyliss, *Tough Love*, Bantam, New York, 1983.

Further Information
(FOR THOSE WHO WORK WITH CHILDREN)

✦

My GOAL IN writing this book is to help parents recognize and eliminate what I call "put-down parenting"–the use of destructive messages as a form of child control. All the chapters following the first are there to provide alternatives to the put-down style, so that parents may relinquish it and not be left at a loss for what to do instead.

Child care and counseling professionals may recognize many of the concepts used in this book; however for those wishing to trace particular ideas to their source, or to explore the implications for helping families and children, a brief summary of sources for each chapter follows:

1. Seeds in the mind

The significance of childhood "taping" of parental messages was first recognized by Eric Berne, and is a central part of the treatment system known as Transactional Analysis. Robert and Mary Goulding systematized the negative programming of children into ten basic "DON'T" messages, and found that it was not passive programming (as Berne had believed), but an "out-of-awareness" cooperation by the child that allowed the messages to remain in action, often severely impairing adult life chances. Tracing and bringing into awareness this programming forms a powerful treatment technique known as "Redecision Therapy."

Children who have been severely deprived and/or disturbed may lack replacement messages even if placed in a caring environment. Jacqui and Aaron Schiff demonstrated success with a system of intensive reprogramming of such children, with highly directive and highly nurturant components, known as "Reparenting."

The concept of "accidental hypnosis" is directly attributable to the work of Milton Erikson, and is described both in his own books and the many books written about him since his death. In particular, Richard Bandler and John Grinder have made clear how this process takes place and also how it can be deliberately used. The ethics of this are currently being debated.

"You-messages" were popularized under that name by Thomas Gordon, in the enormously successful Parent Effectiveness system. Under the name of "attributions" they are discussed in almost any Family Therapy text, for instance books by Virginia Satir, Jay Haley, R. D. Laing, etc.

2. What Children Really Want

The early work of Rene Spitz, John Bowlby and others, and writing on the conditions known as hospitalism and marasmus led to the concept of "positive strokes." The whole behavior modification approach builds on this concept–that "what you stroke is what you get." Amelia Auckett's book on baby massage is a good introduction to affectionate parenting.

3. Curing by Listening

Also known as "Active Listening," this process evolved from Carl Rogers's client-centered counseling, as applied to everyday situations. Once again Thomas Gordon takes credit for making this approach available to parents.

4. Kids and Emotions

Emotions are best understood as variants of the four biological states—anger, fear, sadness, and joy. While these are innate, the expression of them is shaped by familial and cultural factors to an enormous degree. Counseling theory and practice—for instance, ReEvaluation Counseling—is helpful in understanding and freeing up the emotional side of being human. The systematic teaching of expressive and yet socially constructive emotional responses was developed by the Reparenting School of Transactional Analysis. The concept of "racket," or phony, emotions aimed at controling others is an important part of this theory.

5. The Assertive Parent

Assertiveness is widely known and taught, but not often applied directly to parenting. This is a pity because if parents were assertive they would not need to use put-downs. Adequate books and courses on assertiveness deal with the surface skills; the really useful books and courses help parents look at their own negative programming.

The "Tough Love" movement looks very worthwhile for parents with problem kids, though good liaison with professionals is needed for self-help groups to succeed.

6. Family Shape

Margaret Mead, in her irrepressible way, did most to remind us that we no longer live in real families, but in fragments of families. The books of psychologist Mary Pipher, especially *The Shelter of Each Other*, are brilliant descriptions of the lack of community in modern American life, and why people need less therapy and more neighborhood.

7. Ages and Stages

The developmental stages used in this book were based on the work of Pamela Levin. Jean Illsley-Clarke's book (listed in "*References*"), which expands Levin's ideas further, is a useful and down-to-earth child development guide by ages and issues.

8. Energy and How to Save It

The experience of being "drained" by some people, and of giving and receiving energy to and from others, is almost universally acknowledged by parents. The work of Ken Mellor and Julie Henderson and other "bioenergeticists" points to this being more than just a metaphor, and can be lifesaving for those parents for whom exhaustion is a daily hazard. Approaches such as Reiki, massage, meditation, and relaxation can all be invaluable for parents, and should be made routinely available.

About the *Author*

✦

Steve *Biddulph* STARTED out as a family
psychologist in the mid-1970s. Realizing he didn't have a clue,
he traveled and learned from some of the best practitioners in
Australia, the United States, New Zealand, and Singapore during the early days of family therapy. Throughout this time he
worked with hundreds of families in both normal and extreme
situations, and saw the need for more positive and helpful information for parents.

The worldwide success of *The Secret of Happy Children* has led
him to work mostly in parent education. Steve gives talks about
nonviolent discipline, raising boys to be safe men, and other
topics in countries as diverse as Germany, Northern Ireland,
England, and the People's Republic of China, where his books
have been widely translated. He trains therapists in helping people recover from childhood trauma, abuse, and neglect.

Steve and Shaaron now live in the rainforest of Northern
New South Wales, Australia, and in the U.K.. Their wombats are
living their own lives!